HYDE IN HOLLYWOOD

Peter Parnell

BROADWAY PLAY PUBLISHING INC
New York
www.broadwayplaypublishing.com
info@broadwayplaypublishing.com

HYDE IN HOLLYWOOD
© Copyright 1990 Peter Parnell

All rights reserved. This work is fully protected under the copyright laws of the United States of America. No part of this publication may be photocopied, reproduced, stored in a retrieval system, or transmitted, in any form or by any means, electronic, mechanical, recording, or otherwise, without the prior permission of the publisher. Additional copies of this play are available from the publisher.

Written permission is required for live performance of any sort. This includes readings, cuttings, scenes, and excerpts. For amateur and stock performances, please contact Broadway Play Publishing Inc. For all other rights please contact the author c/o B P P I.

First edition: March 1991
This edition: June 2018
I S B N: 978-0-88145-090-3

Book design: Marie Donovan
Page make-up: Adobe InDesign
Typeface: Palatino

HYDE IN HOLLYWOOD was originally coproduced by Playwrights Horizons and American Playhouse Theater Productions, opening on 30 November 1989. The cast and creative contributors were as follows:

JULIAN HYDE	Robert Joy
HOLLYWOOD CONFIDENTIAL	Keith Szarabajka
CHARLES HOCK	Stephen Pearlman
JAKE SINGER	Peter Frechette
DAVID HOGARTH	Robert Curtis-Brown
BETTY ARMSTRONG	Fran Brill
LIDA TODD/SUSAN	Julie Boyd
REYNALDO ROMERO/AGENT	Derek D Smith
BOOKIE/ANDREW/FLORIST	Kurt Deutsch
HARRY SLEZAK/REX MARKUM/ SUGIE SUGARMAN/SENATOR	Herbert Rubens
MOVIE STAR/COSTUME DESIGNER/ FAYE NORRIS/FILM ACTRESS/ STUDIO SECRETARY	Theresa McElwee
RICARDO/ENSEMBLE	Kenneth L Marks
MARTIN/ENSEMBLE	Richard Topol
REPORTERS/FILM CREW/EXTRAS	Thomas Eldon, Thia Gartner, Ed Mahler, Rob Richards

Director	Gerald Gutierrez
Set design	Douglas Stein
Lighting	Frances Aronson
Costumes	Ann Hould-Ward
Sound	Scott Lehrer

To J.M.S. from P.D.P.

CHARACTERS

JULIAN HYDE, film star and director
HOLLYWOOD CONFIDENTIAL, gossip columnist
CHARLES HOCK, studio head
JAKE SINGER, HYDE's screenwriter
DAVID HOGARTH, HYDE's friend, a publicist
BETTY ARMSTRONG, HOLLYWOOD's secretary
LIDA TODD, actress

STUDIO SECRETARY/HARRY SLEZAK/BOOKIE/
BUDDY DAGGERT/REPORTERS/ART DIRECTOR/
COSTUME DESIGNER/REYNALDO ROMERO/
STAGEHAND/FLORIST/SUGIE SUGARMAN/
FAYE NORRIS/FILM CREW/PRESS AGENT/
SENATOR/ACTRESS/RICARDO/ANDREW/
SUSAN/RADIO ANNOUNCER/AUDIO MAN/
LOUELLA PARSON'S VOICE/HEDDA HOPPER'S VOICE/
REX MARKUM/MARTIN

The play takes place in Hollywood in 1939, and at the end in 1959.

AUTHOR'S NOTE

The following version of HYDE IN HOLLYWOOD is a revised text adapted from the version produced by Playwrights Horizons and American Playhouse Theater Productions at the American Place Theater in New York. The New York text has been preserved (with only minor changes) in the *American Playhouse* production shot for PBS in December 1989, and aired on *American Playhouse* in the spring of 1991. The cast for both the stage and television productions was the same.

ACT ONE

(When the play begins, the scrim or upstage mirrors reflect the words HYDE IN HOLLYWOOD.)

(Lights rise on JULIAN HYDE's *movie studio office.* HYDE *is talking to his screenwriter,* JAKE SINGER)

HYDE: I have a secret.

JAKE: Are you a Communist? Jewish? A spy?

HYDE: Take your pick.

JAKE: How about all three?

HYDE: You envy my power and decide to try and find out what my secret is....

JAKE: Or maybe I just find it out by chance.

HYDE: Or maybe it should only *appear* to me to be by chance. Maybe there's something that happened between us, years ago, that links you and me in some clear way, which I have to figure out....

JAKE: And in figuring it out, you find out I have a secret, too.

HYDE: Exactly. So we've got something on each other.

JAKE: And in the end....

HYDE: In the end?

JAKE: Only one of us can be saved....

HYDE: And it has to be me. Because good always triumphs over evil.

JAKE: Says who?

HYDE: God, Franklin Roosevelt, and Louis B. Mayer.

JAKE: But what about life?

HYDE: We're not in life. We're in Hollywood.

JAKE: What makes you think anyone at this Studio can tell the difference?

HYDE: Could it work?

JAKE: Yes, it could work. It *has* worked. It's *been* done. By Joseph Goddamn Conrad, and Edgar Allan Poe.

HYDE: They're both dead.

JAKE: Then they deserve to be out here.

HYDE: Go easy on the hard stuff, Jake. It's only 5:30.

JAKE: That makes it 8:30, Times Square time. A perfect way to start the evening.

HYDE: We still have a lot to do. I have a story meeting with Hock at ten tomorrow and I'm taking Lida to the opening tonight. I hear it's terrible, by the way.

JAKE: Your marriage?

HYDE: The picture.

JAKE: I've seen it. The best part is the first twenty minutes, which are in black and white. When she goes over the rainbow it switches to color.

HYDE: Funny. When I go over the rainbow, that doesn't usually happen to me....

JAKE: Why couldn't I have gotten an assignment like that? Writing dialogue for Munchkins....

HYDE: They don't give those jobs to playwrights.

ACT ONE

JAKE: *Former* playwrights, if you please. It'll be a dozen years at least before Brooks Atkinson will have the pleasure of dropping an axe on something else with my moniker attached to it. It's murder, I tell you. The murder of beauty and talent.

HYDE: There's murder of beauty everywhere you go, Jake. And certainly murder of talent.

JAKE: Speaking of which, you know Greer Garson, don't you? Didn't you think she was the only great thing in that picture we saw last night?

HYDE: Absolutely! I wanted to say goodbye to Mr Chips ten minutes after I met him!

JAKE: You think you could arrange a little dinner for the both of us some night?

HYDE: She's already taken.

JAKE: Not according to Hedda Hopper she ain't.

HYDE: Since when do you believe everything you read? Besides, I have a great idea. Why not bring Marian and the kid out here?

JAKE: Leave Marian and my son out of this! The marriage is over. The romance is dead.

HYDE: You want romance? We've got Venice on Soundstage One! You and Marian want to travel? There's a New England fishing village across the lot, and the Eiffel Tower outside our door! This Studio is the biggest train set two boys from Brooklyn could ever want!

JAKE: You amaze me. You still talk the way you talked seven years ago, when you first came out here. You could convince Kafka to rent a cottage at the Chateau Marmont.

HYDE: Why would I want Kafka when I've got you?

(JAKE *toasts* HYDE. *Intercom buzzes.*)

VOICE: Miss Todd is here.

HYDE: Lida? She's supposed to be shooting....

VOICE: She says she has to see you.

(LIDA TODD *enters. She has a Mary Pickford-innocent quality about her, but is dressed in a Dietrich-type outfit, and is in a state.*)

LIDA: I can't do it, Julian! I can't go on!

HYDE: Lida, for God's sake!

LIDA: He hates me! He dresses like Hitler, and yells at me, and cracks his whip. He calls me his Eva Braun.

HYDE: Look, we've been through all this. You have to go back out there, this must be costing Hock thousands of —

LIDA: Charley doesn't know I'm here.

HYDE: Well, he'll sure as hell figure it out pretty quick.

LIDA: Weiskopf would never call him. Too scared. The little shit. Dresses up like Adolph, but he's a coward through and through. I said it was an emergency. I ran off the set and —

HYDE: Lida, you can't do this. Jake and I are in the middle of an important —

LIDA: And I'm not important?! I'm still your wife, for God's sake! That should count for something, shouldn't it? (*Upset*) How could Charley let Weiskopf put me in this picture? He's got me doing a striptease in front of my *father*! He wants me to kiss some dumb chorus girl on the *lips*! What are my fans going to think? And this dress! (*She looks at herself in the mirror.*) Look at her! Just look! Who does he think I am? Dietrich? (*To* HYDE) You've got to help me, darling. You've got to talk to Charley....

ACT ONE

HYDE: You know I can't do that....

LIDA: You've got to! All it'll take is one little call! They don't understand me! Not like you! You're the only one who does! You understand, don't you, Jake?

JAKE: Sweetheart, just call me Aimee Semple MacPherson.

LIDA: Jake understands. He knows the torment I go through. He knows how it hurts me to even think about....

HYDE: Lida, darling...this is neither the time nor the place.... *(Pause)*

LIDA: I had a dream last night. I dreamt I ran off the set and got in our car and drove it off Pacific Palisades. Thank Christ, I'm finally dead, I thought. But I wasn't. They found me and brought me back. They had to bandage me up from head to toe, like some Egyptian mummy. And when they got me back, they took off my ribbons and I wasn't there. I was like the Invisible Man, remember him?

JAKE: That's my favorite scary picture!

LIDA: And Charley started to yell and yell, 'cause all I was was bandages lying on the floor.... "Where is she?" he shouted. "Where's she gone? We've got three more setups to shoot before six!" And all I could do was laugh and laugh, my laugh sailing all around the studio like Claude What'shisname. Isn't that the best? *(Pause)* I feel so tired, darling.... So tired of all of it....

HYDE: Have they put you on those pills again? Goddamn it, why does the studio doc give them to you?

LIDA: There's a man after me, Julian. There's a man after me, who hates me. Who wants to kill me.

JAKE: A man? What man?

HYDE: Who is this guy? You've never mentioned him....

(She gets up and grabs HYDE.*)*

LIDA: Hold me, darling. You won't let him get us. Will you? You won't let him....

HYDE: Now, calm down, Lida.... *(Pause)* You have to go back on the set, darling. There's only one more—

LIDA: Set up to shoot before six.... *(Pause)* This is the last picture I make, Julie.

HYDE: That's fine.

LIDA: When it's over, I'm going to take a long rest....

HYDE: There, now. I'll pick you up at eight.

*(*LIDA *exits.)*

JAKE: Poor little kid. I hope she gets home alright.

HYDE: It hurts me seing her like this. It's been worse since I moved out.

JAKE: You two should never have gotten married in the first place.

HYDE: I was afraid we'd have to take her to the hospital to pump her stomach. Hedda would have had a field day. You think we'll be able to get her to the opening of *The Wizard of Oz*?

JAKE: I think it's time for me to see the Wizard myself.

HYDE: To ask for a heart?

JAKE: No. Some courage. There's this chorus girl I ran into on the lot this morning who bears an uncanny resemblance to Hedy Lamarr.

HYDE: Jake, you're impossible.

ACT ONE

JAKE: O bright and beautiful California. O bright and beautiful future. Fuck Poland. We're here to make movies!

(He drinks. Immediately the stage becomes filled with activity. A scrim lights up and says: LIDA TODD FOUND BEATEN UNDER HOLLYWOOD SIGN and another that asks: WILL LIDA LIVE? Lights rise on CHARLEY HOCK's *movie studio office.* BUDDY DAGGERT *and a* BOOKIE *are on separate phones.* HARRY SLEZAK *is reading aloud to* HOCK *from a script.)*

SLEZAK: *(Reads)* "Would you prefer to go on as you have, unable to see your shadow in the sunlight, unable to look into a mirror because you know there's nothing there to see...."

BOOKIE: *(On phone)* Killjoy in the first race.

(Phone rings. BUDDY *answers it.)*

SLEZAK: "I should shoot myself first! And I'll shoot you!"

BUDDY: *(To* HOCK*)* It's Louella, Charley.

HOCK: *(Shakes his head)* Tell her I'll call her back in ten.

BOOKIE: Happytalk in the 2nd.

BUDDY: She's asking if she can talk to Julian Hyde.

HOCK: Tell her to check with Bernie Bugle.

BUDDY: She doesn't want to talk to Bernie. No publicists, she says. She wants the dirt straight from the horse's mouth.

BOOKIE: *(On phone)* Place it on Angel Street in the third race, Hecky.

HOCK: Tell her I promise her an exclusive. My word of God. Just ask her to hold off on any dirty stuff on Lida.

BUDDY: Yes, Charley.

HOCK: She's a beautiful gal, tell her.

BUDDY: *Yes*, Sir.

HOCK: And she ain't no sex maniac!

SLEZAK: "...and I'll shoot you!..."

HOCK: *(To nobody in particular)* I can't talk to anybody now. I'm too broken up. There's too much to think about....

BUDDY: She says, no guarantees.

HOCK: Naturally.

BUDDY: She's got to print *something*, she says.

HOCK: They're all scum, these columnists! And she — as God is my witness — is the biggest of them all!

BOOKIE: Hurricane in the fourth.

SLEZAK: "At which point," the script says, "Max takes out a gun and fires. A police whistle is heard. Max fires again and says, 'Die, die, Monster!'"

HOCK: What? Who says this?

SLEZAK: Max Fright.

HOCK: Yeah, but who does he say it to?

SLEZAK: The Monster.

HOCK: I know, I know, but *who* is the Monster?

(HYDE *appears, moving swiftly to* HOCK's *office. He is pursued by* REPORTERS, *one of whom is* HOLLYWOOD CONFIDENTIAL.)

REPORTER #1: Mr Hyde! Did you two have a fight?

REPORTER #2: How is she? Have you seen her?

REPORTER #3: Where were you? Was Lida alone in the house?

ACT ONE

HOLLYWOOD: I wonder if you could tell me, since you were separated from Miss Todd....

(Brief pause)

HYDE: We were — are — not separated.

HOLLYWOOD: What? But Hedda announced in her column last week....

HYDE: We are not separated.

HOLLYWOOD: Can I print that retraction?

(Pause)

HYDE: No. *(Pause)* Look, I'm sorry — I — I can't talk about that right now. If you'll all excuse me....

(He leaves quickly. REPORTERS shout after him. HOLLYWOOD watches him go.)

HOLLYWOOD: I'll be here, Mr Hyde....

(HOCK's intercom buzzes.)

WOMAN'S VOICE: Mr Hyde is here, Mr Hock.

(HYDE enters.)

HOCK: Julian! Christ. We've been looking all over for you!

HYDE: How is she?

HOCK: How do you think? Beaten up and left for dead. And under the Hollywoodland sign, no less. Like a goddamn sacrifice!

(HOCK snaps his fingers.)

HOCK: Alright, everybody. Out. Out.

BOOKIE: Anybody else in?

HOCK: Ask Mr Hyde.

HYDE: I don't bet, Charley.

HOCK: It's on me. Put a cool G on Happytalk for Mr Hyde, Billy. We'll take it out of the budget for his next picture....

(Everybody leaves.)

HOCK: Nothing goes beyond this room, you understand? Alright. Spill. I want to know what happened.

HYDE: I told you this morning. I don't know anything about....

HOCK: You took her to the opening last night.

HYDE: As planned. She loved it, especially the part with the flying monkeys.

HOCK: She seemed nervous after. Jumpy.

HYDE: She was upset about one of her boyfriends.

HOCK: Who's that?

HYDE: I don't know. She doesn't tell me these things.

HOCK: She should. What kind of a husband are you, anyway?

HYDE: Not a very jealous one.

HOCK: What did you do after the picture?

HYDE: I took her home. Then I went — to where I've been staying....

HOCK: Were you followed?

HYDE: I don't think so.

HOCK: Was there anyone in the place when you got there?

HYDE: Not immediately. No. *(Pause)* Are you asking did I sleep alone last night?

HOCK: Of course not. I already know the answer to that one.... *(Pause)* I want you to move to the Wilshire.

ACT ONE

It's near the hospital, and we can say you're stricken with grief and going to visit Lida twice a day. You can't stay where you've been staying, and the reporters are going to be holed up outside your house, anyway. I should have figured something like this would happen....

HYDE: Look, it's wasn't my fault! I take care of her as much as I can! Jesus, who could have done this?

HOCK: Her wedding ring is missing. Whoever took it sure had an appreciation for diamonds....

HYDE: Lida... Poor Lida...

HOCK: We're going to have to square our stories for the press.

HYDE: The press! Always the press!

HOCK: Damn right, the press! Until Hedda broke that story, everybody thought you were happily married!

HYDE: Thanks to you and Bernie Bugle!

HOCK: Our publicist has to run the columnists around somehow, doesn't he? Jesus, you don't make his job easy!

(HOCK *sinks into a chair. Rubs his eyes.*)

HOCK: What a year it's been. First Harry Haynes and that Andre girl on cocaine charges, then Marie Kendall gets eaten by a bear.

HYDE: A what?

HOCK: A bear. On the set of *Canadian Campfire*.

HYDE: Oh.

HOCK: And now this—my number one starlet goes too heavy on the S&M sauce.... You'd think these people would be grateful to be making so much money while the rest of the country's finally come out of a Depression. A girl like Lida— an ordinary kid who we took out of a mob scene in front of Grauman's Chinese Theater and made into a star! It isn't just her lack of professionalism. It upsets me personally! *(Pause. He says simply, genuinely.)* Jesus...I hope she's going to be all right....

(HOCK's *intercom buzzes.)*

WOMAN'S VOICE: Mr DeMarco calling from Lot 12.

HOCK: *(On the phone)* Tommy? Tell Weiskopf he shouldn't stop shooting. *Her Naughty Ways* has to finish in two weeks.... Well, shoot around her, then.... I just talked to her doctor.... Lida will be fine.... We'll get her up and out of that hospital bed if we have to drag her! *(Puts down phone. Rubs his eyes.)* Where are those drops?

HYDE: I'll do it.

HOCK: Be gentle. They sting like hell.

(HYDE *puts drops in* HOCK's *eyes.)*

HYDE: I thought about you this morning, Charley. Gave me an idea for a story.

HOCK: Jesus. How can you think about movies at a time like this?

HYDE: Movies are all I ever think about, you know that. A blind man gets an operation, and is given the eyes of a dead man. He sees for the first time. But the dead man was murdered, and the eyes recognize the murderer, who pursues the poor blind man before he goes to the police.

HOCK: Sounds great. What happens?

HYDE: I haven't figured the rest out yet. *(Pause)* Maybe the murderer puts poison in the blind man's eye drops.

ACT ONE 13

(HOCK *splutters as the drops go in, and leans on the desk. Hands over his eyes.*)

HOCK: You've sure got a strange sense of humor.

HYDE: "And how are the story conferences on your picture going, Julian? Very well, thank you, Charley...."

HOCK: Your picture! That's all I ever hear about is the great Julian Hyde's next picture!

HYDE: Sometimes you slay me.

HOCK: Who are you, the Pope?

HYDE: No. But I give this Studio a little class. A little prestige.

HOCK: Class? Prestige? Who do you think we are, Paramount?

HYDE: You need me! I win Oscars for you! Like Cohn needs Capra, Hock needs Hyde!

HOCK: And what about you? Don't you need us? You think you could get such a deal by walking across the street?! Complete artistic control, writing, acting, directing, unheard of in Hollywood, and you're complaining?! When have you ever not gotten what you wanted — and at what price?!

HYDE: I've gotten it because I deserve it —

HOCK: YES you deserve it, but do WE deserve YOU?

HYDE: What do you mean?

HOCK: That Napoleon epic you made —

HYDE: *The Eagle Beheaded* —

HOCK: *Eagle Beheaded* — there were scenes in that thing — magnificent, Julian, I *wept* at the preview, you saw me, I wept.... But all that footage you never used, that entire battlefield scene cut from the story!

HYDE: I couldn't use it, the way Beekman shot it....

HOCK: And that Nazi thriller, *Stranger in the Shadows* — it took three different art directors before —

HYDE: Okay, so I'm difficult! I am, and always have been! That's because I want and demand the best! The last couple of projects haven't been all aces, but neither has the creative team — *your* creative team. That's why I've brought in Jake Singer.

HOCK: Jake Singer — a writer like that you call a winner?

HYDE: He's the first writer I ever worked with. He wrote *Face in the Moonlight*, didn't he?

HOCK: Yeah, and then he went back to New York!

HYDE: Because you threw him off the lot for having an egg cream with Upton Sinclair!

HOCK: He had more than an egg cream with that Red! He voted for him!

HYDE: Sinclair wasn't a Red, for God's sake, he was — oh, forget it!

HOCK: So far this thing sounds like a psychological suspense pic about a guy being chased by his shadow.

HYDE: It's not as simple as that. Its themes go as far back as E.T.A. Hoffmann.

HOCK: Who's Hoffmann?

HYDE: German writer. Remember *The Nutcracker Suite*?

HOCK: He wrote that?

HYDE: Based on his story.

HOCK: He ever visit California?

HYDE: He'd dead, Charley.

HOCK: Too bad. I'd rather give him a grand a week. Plus he'd help sell this story to the overseas market.

HYDE: The important relationships are between the two men.

HOCK: The guy and the other guy.

HYDE: The pursuer and the pursued...

HOCK: The good guy and the bad guy...

HYDE: There's a subtlety to the relationships, one is neither all good, nor the other all evil, but they're possessed, the masks of good and evil, light and dark keep shifting....

HOCK: Alright, alright! Look, I'm putting a lot of money behind this one — you know I'm counting on you with it, Son! Just get rolling, so we've got something to tell the press besides where you were when you heard about Lida....

(Pause)

HYDE: We created her, Charley. Remember that amazing night? The night we discovered her?

HOCK: I sure do....

HYDE: She was terrific in her first picture. There was a quality about her, everybody's all-American girl. But then...I don't know what happened. Whether it's the pictures she's been making, or her own success.... It's begun to feel like an act. Like her whole life has become unreal, and there's another side to her....

HOCK: She's never talked to you about it?

HYDE: She won't, no matter how much I ask. She's like a kid who just wants to forget. Ever since Lucy Tekosky became Lida Todd, it's as if Lucy has never existed. As if she's been running away from herself in picture after picture. *(Pause)* It feels like she's been running for the past three years....

(Pause)

HOCK: Look, I'll talk to the police. You just lie low for a few days and let Bernie handle the press. And for God's sake, stay out of trouble!

HYDE: I always do....

(HYDE leaves. Intercom buzzes.)

WOMAN'S VOICE: It's the hospital calling, Mr Hock.

HOCK: Put them on.

(HYDE passes HOLLYWOOD.)

HOCK: Hello?... I see.... God... Jesus... Yes...

HOLLYWOOD: Mr Hyde?

HYDE: Oh. It's you.

HOLLYWOOD: Confidential. Hollywood Confidential. We met once, a few years ago. Don't you remember?

HYDE: I'm sorry, I....

HOLLYWOOD: You don't remember, do you. *(Pause)* I wonder if you could take a minute to....

HYDE: I'm sorry. Not now.

HOLLYWOOD: Some friends of Lida's said she liked to go to the Cafe Gala.

(Pause)

HYDE: The what?

HOLLYWOOD: The Cafe Gala. Above Sunset.

HYDE: What's the matter with that?

HOLLYWOOD: After midnight, I mean. It's...a pretty risqué place....

ACT ONE

HYDE: Who told you that?

HOLLYWOOD: That it's risqué?

HYDE: No. The other thing. About Lida.

HOLLYWOOD: Somebody named Jim Doyle.

HYDE: I'm sorry. I don't know him.

HOLLYWOOD: Are you sure? Jimmy Doyle?

(Pause)

HYDE: I'm sure.

HOLLYWOOD: Yeah, well. I didn't figure you would. Him purportedly being a yoo-hoo boy.

HYDE: A what?

HOLLYWOOD: You know. A homosexualist. They say Lida has many close friends who are homosexualists. Did you know that?

HYDE: *(Coolly)* No, Mr Confidential. I didn't.

HOLLYWOOD: Yeah, well... Have a good day, Mr Hyde.

(HYDE *exits, as* HOLLYWOOD *watches after him.*)

HOCK: *(On phone)* Bernie. Call Lot 12. Have production stopped on *Her Naughty Ways*. Tell DeMarco that Lida Todd just died. And call Musso's for a reuben. I'll be eating in.

(HOCK *slumps in his seat. Puts his face in his hands. Lights dim on* HOCK's *office as* HOLLYWOOD *goes to his office. Slide on scrim changes to another headline: ORGY OF BLOOD—WHEN WILL IT STOP? and another saying WHO KILLED LIDA?* HOLLYWOOD *enters.* BETTY, HOLLYWOOD's *secretary, is on the phone.*)

BETTY: Yes, Chief, I'll tell him.... He just walked in....

HOLLYWOOD: Is that Eddie? *(*BETTY *nods.)* Tell him I'm on a lead.

(He exits.)

BETTY: Oh, dear, he just walked out again.... Right... Bye...

(BETTY hangs up. HOLLYWOOD pokes his head in.)

HOLLYWOOD: He gone?

BETTY: Cute. The Chief wants more dirt on the Lida Todd story.

HOLLYWOOD: Tell him to shove it.

BETTY: He wants more punch in the copy.

HOLLYWOOD: I'll punch *him*.

BETTY: And as much as you can on the sex angle. He says that's what'll keep them reading.

HOLLYWOOD: That's for sure.

BETTY: Oh, and he wants....

BOTH: A little sermonizing, too...

BETTY: And Bernie Bugle called a few minutes ago. I guess you heard.

HOLLYWOOD: It's all over the street.

BETTY: He read me a statement. Said her last words were "I love you, Julian.... Good luck on your new picture...."

HOLLYWOOD: How touching! Ben Hecht couldn't have written it better!

(He picks up pieces of paper.)

HOLLYWOOD: This press agent stuff?

BETTY: Been coming in all day.

HOLLYWOOD: Anything good?

(BETTY shakes her head.)

HOLLYWOOD: Jesus, when are folks gonna start taking me serious in this town?! *(Reads)* On again off again with Betty Grable and Jackie Coogan.... Let's say it's on again.... Harry Ormond suggests something's looming with Greer Garson and Richard Ney.... *(He checks through papers.)* SEE HOPPER COLUMN LAST MONTH.... *(He goes through pages.)* Wrongo. Oh, I know, mention Garson in the same breath with Cary Grant drinking problem. "WAS CARY GRANT DOWNING A FEW TOO MANY AT THE BROWN DERBY? CERTAINLY HAD HIS GOOD LOOKS...." It wasn't, make a note it was Lou Alcar, and I'll put in later in the week that he's a Grant look-alike headed for possible superstardom.... Don't print apology to Grant, though, unless we hear from his office....

BETTY: When have we ever heard from Grant's office?

HOLLYWOOD: Christ, Betty, whose side are you on? "AND SPEAKING OF DOWNING A FEW, PERHAPS GREER GARSON HAS GIVEN SOBER CONSIDERATION TO HER RICHARD NEY ROMANCE FOLLOWING HER BEHAVIOR AT THE JOAN FONTAINE WEDDING...." If Garson calls, send her a dozen roses.

(BETTY cackles. Phone rings. He picks it up.)

HOLLYWOOD: Hollywood Confidential... Yeah, Sunny, I got your stuff.... It's lousy.... I can't do anything with Crawford, Hedda's been running on her all week.... Why don't you give me the ace stuff, like you give Hedda? Of course I ain't Hedda, that's the point! If there were more than two big hacks in this town, we'd all be better off.... Did I know Katherine Hepburn has a head cold? No, but tell her to take two aspirins and call me in the morning. *(He makes a note.)* ...If she sees a doctor, I'll put it in.... *(Pause)* I just heard the news about Lida.... Oh, suddenly you clam up.... I know she wasn't your client, but still, you hear things, don't you?... Why was Hyde staying with Metro publicist David Hogarth during the trial separation?... I know they're old friends.... Sure, I'd talk to Hogarth, but he won't return any of my calls!... What do you mean, you can't talk now, Claudette Colbert is calling?! I hear she's been pretty palsy lately with Marlene.... *(Laughs)* What do you mean, I can't print that? Wanna make a bet!? *(He hangs up.)* Christ, I need some kind of angle.

BETTY: You find anything out?

HOLLYWOOD: The studio's shut tight as a drum. Hock's not saying a word. Every two-bit actor claims to have known her, but nobody's giving me any hard facts.

BETTY: What about Hyde?

HOLLYWOOD: Wouldn't talk. He seemed very upset.

BETTY: 'Course he was upset. They were Hollywood's dream couple.

HOLLYWOOD: There ain't no such thing as a dream couple in Hollywood, Betty.

BETTY: Remember the famous story of how she and Hyde first met?

HOLLYWOOD: I remember all right....

BETTY: Grauman's...opening night of *Stranger in the Shadows*. Hyde's co-star Barbara Sherwood took sick, and Hyde needed a date for the night, so he pulled her out of the crowd. Lucy, wasn't that her real name? Lucy....

HOLLYWOOD: Tekosky. Lucy Tekosky...

BETTY: She became his greatest discovery. It was like watching two gods....

ACT ONE

HOLLYWOOD: Gods! If I've taught you anything, Betty, it's that in this business, there are no gods! There are only little stick figures trying not to fall! Little Pinocchios hoping nobody sees their noses are too long! Everybody's hiding something, understand? Everybody's hiding something.... *(Phone rings.* HOLLYWOOD *jumps on it.)* Hollywood Confidential... Hi, Sid... Thanks for the scoop on Coop... Did I see Conrad Nagel holding hands with who at the Trocadero?... No, but I did know.... Listen, Sid, I'm gonna do a clean-up on Hollywood.... I'm taking a hard line.... What can you tell me about the swishy boys Lida Todd spent time with?... DESPERATE? I AIN'T DESPERATE! Alright, well, you hear anything, America wants to know! *(He hangs up.)* Christ.

BETTY: Stomach hurt again?

HOLLYWOOD: Must be this bromo I'm taking. For my stomach. Ulcer or something.

BETTY: Never sick a day in your life.

HOLLYWOOD: Must be the food I ate. Bad food.

BETTY: Oh, I nearly forgot. The hat-check girl at the Zenda Room called.

HOLLYWOOD: What'd she want?

BETTY: Said she'd meet you at the Palomar Lounge at seven.

HOLLYWOOD: Got a bright future, that kid. But she's also got a slight jealousy problem. She thinks I chase every skirt in town.

BETTY: Don't you?

HOLLYWOOD: 'Course not.

(Pause)

BETTY: HC? Is it true what you just told Sid? About taking a hard line?

HOLLYWOOD: What if it is?

BETTY: Nothing. I just never heard you talk like that before.

HOLLYWOOD: It's about time somebody took on the big guys who tolerate the pornographic peccadilloes of the Hollywood Hot Set.

(Phone rings. BETTY *picks up.)*

BETTY: Hollywood Confidential... Oh, yes, Mr Harrell...

*(*HOLLYWOOD *grabs the phone.)*

HOLLYWOOD: Hi, Eddie... Listen, what do you mean, telling me what to write? What? Sure I've got a scoop.... I can't tell you it just yet, but I promise it's big.... She liked the rough stuff, old Lida.... They think it was an extra she was playing with, off the set of *Her Naughty Ways*.... Oh, and the best, she loved the swishy boys, too.... Got that from some fairy who hangs out at the Gala.... No, no names just yet... I'll write it up good, don't you worry.... This could be the biggest thing since von Stroheim's weekends in Sodom.... Right... *(He hangs up.)* What a loser.

BETTY: You're telling me.

HOLLYWOOD: Alright. Take this down. SINS OF THE CITY... Lida Todd, the Goddess of Goddesses, was, according to some Babylon Babblers, the most notorious of the beat-me-but-good school of fun times, and nobody could stop her.... But did anybody really try? Where were the boys in the front office on the night of August the 15th?... Lapping their liquor at more wild parties in Pictureland, no doubt.... Right now, there's no BADDER place in this fine country

ACT ONE

than the strip of land called HOLLYWOOD bordered by Santa Monica-Sodom and Glendale-Gomorrah on each side, and it doesn't take an Einstein of Innuendo to guess who is doing most of the sinning....

BETTY: And what sinning there is!

HOLLYWOOD: And what—exactly—sinning, etc., etc. Drink, drugs—no, dope, — and debauchery, sex, suicide, murder, and you guessed it, the worst of all — PERVERSIONS, including those involving secretive members of the so-called "third sex"... many of whom numbered themselves among Lida's best friends....

BETTY: Stop the presses.

HOLLYWOOD: We'll move that to the top.

BETTY: Above "lapping their liquor"...

HOLLYWOOD: ...And who, according to one young man, J.D., a well-known chorus-singer in the twenties tear-jerker *Backstreet Baby*, enjoyed tangoing their tawdry little hearts out with her at such late-night hot spots as the Club Gala above Sunset Strip....

BETTY: You want this in caps?

HOLLYWOOD: Not yet. *(Phone rings.)* Hold.

BETTY: *(On phone)* Hollywood Confidential, hold please.

HOLLYWOOD: ...AND WHOSE NUMBERS INCLUDE AT LEAST TWO FORMER WELL-KNOWN STARS OF THE SILENT SCREEN, A CURRENT SCREEEN IDOL, AND ONE OF THE BIGGEST LEADING LADIES OF OUR TIME....

BETTY: There we go, in caps....

HOLLYWOOD: More to follow tomorrow, etc., etc.

BETTY: Kiddo, that's a peach! *(On phone)* Hollywood Confidential... Oh, hello... Yes, he's right here....

(She hands HOLLYWOOD *the phone.)*

HOLLYWOOD: Yeah... Yeah... Yeah, right... Sweetie, I can't now.... I'm on a lead.... I'll see you at seven.... Yeah... Right... *(He hangs up.)* Always interrupting my train of thought.

BETTY: She's got needs.

HOLLYWOOD: Tell me about it.

BETTY: Is that all then?

HOLLYWOOD: Yeah. Thirty. *(Pause)* Dinner Thursday?

BETTY: What?

HOLLYWOOD: Do you want to have dinner Thursday?

BETTY: Yeah. Sure. I'll — I'll think about it.

(Pause. HOLLYWOOD *looks out the window.)*

HOLLYWOOD: Hollywood and Vine. The two most famous names in the history of the world. Look at it down there. Looks like a movie set, doesn't it? Like the fall of Rome. Every brunette, blonde, and knockout redhead wishing she could have been Lida Todd. Wishing she could have been taking too much dope, drinking too much booze, sleeping with too many men. Wishing she could have the problems of Lida Todd. Lida's got problems, and we want to know about them. We want to know, you can hear the people say. We want to know.... *(Pause)* It's cool, in the night air. Driving up, into the hills. Looking down into the Valley. The city sparkles. Lies spread out before you. Like one big bed. To lie down in. A giant bed to spread yourself out in. Let's take a drive up there. In the twilight. Huh?

BETTY: *(Laughs)* You're crazy.

ACT ONE

HOLLYWOOD: I'm not. Let's take a drive.

(He grabs her. There is something strong between them. HOLLYWOOD *turns away. Phone rings.)*

HOLLYWOOD: Leave it. It's nighttime.

BETTY: You've got Miss Zenda Room. And then that screening.

HOLLYWOOD: Yeah. What is it?

BETTY: *Happy Go Lucky.* Rudy Vallee, Dolores Del Rio. *(Pause)* I'd better go.

(She leaves. HOLLYWOOD *watches her, then looks out the window. To himself, quietly:)*

HOLLYWOOD: *Stranger in the Shadows...*

(Lights fade on HOLLYWOOD *and rise on* HYDE *as he appears walking past flats on the soundstage where the set for his movie is being built. He is followed by* JAKE *and an* ART DIRECTOR *and a* COSTUME DESIGNER. *He carries a bouquet of flowers and is talking on the telephone.)*

HYDE: The bastards! Look, Bernie, you're my publicist, tell them the truth — no, don't do that, make something up! Isn't that what publicists do?... Does Hock want me to talk to these bums?... Well, find out from him, and don't call me back! *(He hangs up.)* Goddamn them! Reporters!

JAKE: It's positively un-American, what they can say about you, isn't it?

HYDE: Don't be sarcastic! Why should they be able to write that Lida and I were both having affairs?

JAKE: You want them to just say she was?

HYDE: I don't want them to say anything!

JAKE: Well, now, that would be asking too much. You are in the public eye, after all. Of course, if you ever get a chance to give it a poke, let me know.

ART DIRECTOR: Julian...

HYDE: *(Looking at rendering)* No, this still isn't right! How much of the castle is going to be constructed?

ART DIRECTOR: Everything from the second flight up, including the central tower, will be small models photographed against the actual structure. We'll just have to precision match for the long shots.

HYDE: And the set for the belfry?

ART DIRECTOR: We'll build it separately.

HYDE: So when Horace chases Harold up the tower....

ART DIRECTOR: We'll intercut. And you can shoot the scene in deep focus like you want.

HYDE: I don't like the fireplace. English Gothic Revival?

ART DIRECTOR: Yeah, but I was thinking of throwing a Farnese Hercules in here or there.

HYDE: And maybe a Bamberg Rider, something Germanic, too.

ART DIRECTOR: How much of the tower will you want lit?

HYDE: There should be as much dark as there is light. The characters should move in and out of light and dark all the time. *(Looking at costume designs)* Don't make Horace's masquerade costume too Egyptian. And I've been thinking, maybe Sarah shouldn't dress so Chinese in that scene, either.

JAKE: *(To* COSTUME DESIGNER*)* Julian tells me you're the lady responsible for putting Ingrid Bergman in that strapless gown in *Intermezzo*.

ACT ONE 27

COSTUME DESIGNER: She certainly didn't resist.

JAKE: And for that, I am eternally grateful.

HYDE: Alright, you two! Good work! See you both tomorrow!

(They leave.)

JAKE: I congratulate you on your technical staff. I particularly admire your costume designer's special effects. *(Pause)* Who sent the buds?

HYDE: An admirer.

JAKE: Known to you, and simply staying unknown to me?

HYDE: You know who it is. Beautiful, aren't they?

JAKE: To birthdays!

HYDE: Yours, not mine. I've been thinking, maybe we shouldn't make Horace a politician.

JAKE: Why not?

HYDE: It's been done. We should find a new way to deal with the nature of evil. What about if we make him a business tycoon? Tell the story from several points of view?

JAKE: Sturges tried it. Didn't work for him.

HYDE: Anyway, I don't like these new pages.

JAKE: Why not?

HYDE: What's all this crap about fascism?

JAKE: It isn't crap. I just thought, as Horace becomes more powerful, we can make a comment on the demon within us that, on a collective level, can lead to the rise of a Franco, a Mussolini, or worse —

HYDE: I'm not interested in filming a political allegory, Jake —

JAKE: No. Only in shooting something that *looks* new and fresh and different!

HYDE: I am interested in human nature — in characters that matter — in telling a good story and in telling it well!

JAKE: That's fine, as long as there'll be people around to enjoy it!

HYDE: Oh, there'll be people all right! Right now, in this year, the voice of Hollywood is the most powerful voice in the world.

JAKE: And what does it speak? Baby talk!

HYDE: And you think you can change that?

JAKE: So did you, once!

HYDE: Look, I've tried more than anybody in this town to make meaningful pictures.

JAKE: Did try! Before you got scared!

HYDE: Scared? Of what?

JAKE: Success! Failure! I don't know! You tell me!

HYDE: By God, you do know how to get my blood boiling....

JAKE: Isn't that why you sent for me? *(Pause)* By the way, have you *seen* Ingrid Bergman in *Intermezzo*?

HYDE: Of course not.

JAKE: But you know her, don't you? I was wondering if maybe you could arrange a little dinner party, some night....

(Pause. HYDE *looks troubled.)*

JAKE: What is it?

HYDE: I keep thinking about Lida. Why did I do it, Jake? Why did I ever take her out of that crowd?

ACT ONE

JAKE: You only cast her in her first picture — you didn't start her on the booze and the pills.

HYDE: I agreed to marry her, didn't I?

JAKE: Well, nobody ever said *that* was a good idea!

HYDE: But Charley insisted! And Lida was in love with me! It seemed good for everybody all around....

JAKE: Everybody except you, you mean. *(Pause)* Have you ever thought about what you'd do if you woke up one day and they said you couldn't make pictures anymore?

HYDE: They? They who?

JAKE: Whoever they are...who decide these things.

HYDE: Nobody decides these things. *(Pause)* No. I never have. *(Pause)* Why?

(REYNALDO ROMERO rushes in. An Italian prettyboy lover type. He carries a rolled-up news tabloid with him.)

REYNALDO: Julian! Excuse, please.

HYDE: Reynaldo! What are you doing....

REYNALDO: The most terrible news! The Studio! They will fire me!

HYDE: What?

REYNALDO: They will revoke my contract!

HYDE: But... Why...?

(He hands JAKE the newspaper. JAKE opens it and reads.)

JAKE: "PRETTY BOY REYNALDO ROMERO HOLLYWOOD'S LATEST PINK POWDER PUFF!"

REYNALDO: Listen to this! Just listen!

JAKE: *(Reads)* "In his latest Latin-lover pic, pretty-boy Romero is the most effeminate leading man to wow the American woman since the Sheik himself cast

Rambova's slave bracelet into the ring of superstardom! Where are the 'real men' of today? How long will the public put up with this outrage?"

(REYNALDO *paces back and forth.*)

REYNALDO: You hear this? An outrage! "Effeminate leading man"! "Not since Valentino himself..." This is only my second picture, and already they are after me! I am ruined! Ruined!

(REYNALDO, *truly shaken, begins to weep.*)

HYDE: Who wrote this? *(Looks at paper)* Hollywood Confidential! Of course! Jesus, why won't he let up?!

JAKE: They were talking about him at the Troc last night.

HYDE: Haven't you been reading him? He's become powerful quite suddenly. Syndicated in all of Eddie Harrell's newspapers. He's launched a hate campaign targeting Reds and homosexuals.

REYNALDO: He talk about you in this as well.

HYDE: What?

(HYDE *grabs newspaper from* JAKE. *Reads.*)

HYDE: "Insiders still won't say where Julian Hyde was the night of Lida Todd's murder. Word is he never came home at all. Who is the mystery person Hyde has been seeing? Why won't he talk about their relationship?"

(HYDE *goes to the telephone and dials.*)

HYDE: *(On phone)* It's Hyde, is he there?... Bernie, for God's sake, what is going on?!... Yes, I just saw the late edition!... How can he print that? I'm going to call him up, and.... Keep quiet, why should I keep quiet?... But I won't let myself be intimidated!... And you tell Charley I'm creating a special role in my picture for

ACT ONE

Reynaldo Romero.... What do you mean?... Oh, really... Well, I suggest you call Hock back before you do that, and tell him what I just told you.... I don't care what Charley says, I'm putting him in it! *(He hangs up.)* Stupid fools!

REYNALDO: You see? What did I tell you? They are going to drop me.

HYDE: No, they won't. I won't allow it.

JAKE: Look, Mr Romero. I wouldn't worry. These guys' barks are always worse than their bites. *(Pause)* Well, I... better get back to the keyboard.... End of the day, isn't it.

HYDE: Yes. Sunset...

JAKE: Happy birthday, Julian... *(No response. To* REYNALDO:*)* See you on the set, I hope....

REYNALDO: Yes, I...hope so, too....

*(*JAKE *leaves. The area has quieted down. Brief pause.)*

REYNALDO: That was very brave, what you just did for me, Julie....

*(*HYDE *turns violently to* REYNALDO.*)*

HYDE: How dare you come here!

REYNALDO: I'm sorry. I...

HYDE: You must never — *never* — disturb me while I'm working, you understand?

REYNALDO: I was too upset....

HYDE: That makes no difference!

REYNALDO: I thought you were alone!

HYDE: I am never alone! Not here! You know what goes on all around here!

REYNALDO: I had to talk to somebody! I'm sorry! Please!

(REYNALDO *begins to weep.* STAGEHAND *walks by.)*

STAGEHAND: Goodnight, Mr Hyde.

HYDE: Thank you. Good night. *(Pause.* HYDE *calms down.)* It's alright, Rey. I'm sorry. It's over now. *(Pause)* Feeling better?

REYNALDO: No. I feel so alone.

HYDE: You're not. You're here with me.

REYNALDO: You know what I mean.

HYDE: No. I don't

REYNALDO: Not a man. Not a man. What am I supposed to do to prove that I am a man? Make love to a woman?

HYDE: That might be a good start.

REYNALDO: I need you. To protect me.

HYDE: I can't now, Rey. We are in this — each of us — on his own. Besides, I made a promise to David.

REYNALDO: David! Always David! *(Pause)* You did tell the police you were with David the night of Lida's death, didn't you.

HYDE: I had no choice. I had to.

REYNALDO: The Studio will protect you, won't it? You are too valuable to them....

HYDE: I'm only valuable to them as long as I make a successful picture.

(Pause)

REYNALDO: Even if they will have me back...I cannot act anymore.

HYDE: What?

ACT ONE

REYNALDO: I cannot! Not after what they will be saying about me!

HYDE: Listen to me. Do you know what it has been like for me? I've gotten to where I am in spite of what I am. And I'm not going to let anybody take it away from me. And you — you must do the same....

REYNALDO: But how...?

HYDE: You will work hard. Extra hard. Harder than ever before. And you will be better than you have ever been. You will do it. You will show them all. You will be...magnificent.

(REYNALDO *sniffles.* HYDE *embraces him.*)

HYDE: There, now. You should leave. Hock said he'd be stopping by, and I don't think it would be good for him to see you like this.

REYNALDO: Thank you, Julian. For being my friend. How do I look?

HYDE: Like Valentino himself.

REYNALDO: Don't say that. Say like a man.

HYDE: Like a man.

REYNALDO: Like a real man.

HYDE: Like a real man.

(REYNALDO *goes. Turns and blows* HYDE *a kiss. He leaves.* HYDE *stands alone. He is suddenly rather frightened. He turns around, and sees a young man staring at him.*)

FLORIST: Sir? Are you all right?

HYDE: Oh. Yes... It's you....

FLORIST: Sir?

HYDE: Sometimes...in these huge places...

FLORIST: It can seem spooky, can't it.... *(Pause)* I've never been on a soundstage before.

HYDE: You haven't? I'll show you around.

FLORIST: You did say...to come back...after six o'clock....

HYDE: What? Oh. Yes. Sunset. *(Pause)* Thanks for bringing the freesia. They're my favorite, you know. *(Pause)* It's my birthday, you see.

FLORIST: Yes. *(Pause)* Happy birthday.

(Pause. HYDE sniffs the flowers. Looks at the FLORIST. They stand facing each other. Lights go down on them. Slide on scrim of a gossip headline says: ROZ SEES JUNGLE RED! The lights come up on the Zanzibar Lounge of the Conga Club, a nightclub with a tropical jungle atmosphere.)

SUGIE: Good evening, ladies and gentlemen. I am your host Harry "Sugie" Sugarman welcoming you to the opening night gala of Metro-Goldwyn-Mayer's *The Women*. I invite you to dance to the topical tropical step of Dave the Beachcomber and his Tailless Monkeys....

(DAVID HOGARTH appears under the arch. HYDE appears.)

HYDE: Looking for someone?

DAVID: What the — what are you doing here?

HYDE: I beg your pardon. Aren't I on the list? I'm letting myself be seen, for once.

DAVID: But why here?

HYDE: At the Club Conga? I love the Club Conga. Brings out the beast in me. Any place Lupe likes, I like. *(Pause)* Besides, I knew you'd be here. It's your picture, after all.

ACT ONE

DAVID: You're not drunk, are you?

HYDE: Only slightly. My courage needed screwing up. *(Pause)* You look good.

DAVID: So do you.

HYDE: No, I don't. I look terrible.

DAVID: You never look terrible. Tired, maybe.

HYDE: I'm in preproduction. You know what that's like. Fighting all day, scared all night...

DAVID: Yes...I know....

HYDE: And lonely all the time... *(Pause)* How's the house?

DAVID: Still standing.

HYDE: And the dogs?

DAVID: They miss you. I don't know why. You never pay them nearly enough attention.

HYDE: I don't pay them any attention.

DAVID: No. They're furious at being left. They leave the room whenever I mention your name. They're going to do something nasty to you as soon as you're back home. Whenever *that* will be.... *(Pause)* There's Madame Shearer. I really must go.

HYDE: Oh, stay. She can take care of herself.

DAVID: I just don't want her to run into Roz. They're still not speaking to each other.

HYDE: Let them scratch each other's eyes out! Perfect for Louella's column tomorrow. What else have they got to write about with this picture? No back-lot romances, after all!

DAVID: At least, none that are socially acceptable, anyway....

HYDE: I read about your Nazi star in Edith Gwynn's column yesterday.

DAVID: I *begged* her not to print! Of course, he asked for it. Who the hell walks around wearing an armband on the M-G-M lot? I thought Mayer himself was going to have a fit, but he didn't say a word.

HYDE: He and Hock, those guys are all alike. They turn their backs as soon as there's any trouble.

DAVID: Mayer's worse than Charley ever was.

HYDE: If you're that unhappy, I'm sure Charley would have you back in a minute.

DAVID: You must be kidding. Aren't you the reason we all decided I should leave the Studio in the first place?

(FAYE NORRIS, *a glamorous young actress, appears. Moves to* HYDE.)

FAYE: There you are! I thought I'd lost you!

HYDE: Faye, do you know David Hogarth?

FAYE: Oh, no, but I've heard a lot about him.

DAVID: Publicists aren't supposed to be heard from at all, Miss Norris.

FAYE: They say you're quite a whiz at what you do.

HYDE: David is the wunderkind of the press biz, Faye.

FAYE: Congratulations. I hear this picture's terrific.

DAVID: It is. Though my favorite of ours this year is still *Ninotchka*.

HYDE: Very smart, but the politics is spoon-fed to the audience.

DAVID: Since when have you started caring about politics?

ACT ONE

HYDE: Since lately, I guess. Since I feel as if the country has reached its civilized peak, and is now about to go sliding not so gently down into the sea. Are there any other crypto-Fascists on the dance floor?

DAVID: Oh, lots. More than you'd believe. You find out the strangest things when you're a publicist. Not that people tell you, exactly. But they do, after a while, start to think of you as something like their maiden aunt.

HYDE: Especially you, David!

DAVID: I resent that! With three drinks in me, I'm still butcher than half the men at the Studio!

HYDE: And not nearly as butch as half the women!

(They laugh.)

FAYE: Well, I think I'll sidle over to the bar.

HYDE: I'll see you there in a minute.

(FAYE leaves.)

DAVID: She seems quite lovely.

HYDE: She is. Talented, too.

DAVID: Maybe you should marry her.

HYDE: What!? Why?

DAVID: It'll make Hock very happy.

HYDE: Do you think all I care about is making Hock happy?

DAVID: Isn't it?

HYDE: Bernie Bugle insisted. My first night out since Lida's death. Besides, we're probably going to cast her....

DAVID: Exactly.

(Pause)

HYDE: I've tried calling you. Late at night. You're never home.

DAVID: I'm there. I just don't pick up.

HYDE: Why not?

DAVID: Because I don't know what I'd say.

HYDE: Nothing, at first. I'd talk; you'd listen. You'd talk; I'd....

DAVID: Look, I don't like any of this, Julian....

HYDE: Of course you don't. You think I do? But there's no other way, until things die down....

DAVID: And just when will that be?

HYDE: How should I know? For God's sake, you of all people — you're on the front lines with this more than I am....

DAVID: I know that. But we always said, we wouldn't let it get to us....

HYDE: And we won't if we just stay strong.

DAVID: How can we stay strong when we haven't seen each other in weeks? The world is changing faster than we are. If I grab you, I don't know how we'll hold on. *(Pause)* I miss you. I miss holding you at night. I miss waking up to your mishegas.

HYDE: I miss your terrible Yiddish.

DAVID: What else do you miss?

HYDE: I miss — lots of things. *(Pause)* Don't you love this music?

DAVID: Maybe we should hold each other and start swaying. Give Mary Boland a heart attack.

HYDE: Ask Cukor to cut in. *(They laugh.)* To hell with Hollywood!

ACT ONE

(HOLLYWOOD CONFIDENTIAL *comes in, in high spirits. He is changed since we last saw him — more confident.* DAVID *immediately goes to him.*)

HOLLYWOOD: A terrific party, Mr Hogarth!

DAVID: Why, thanks, HC! Er— have you met —

HYDE: *(Icy)* Mr Confidential...

HOLLYWOOD: Hello, Mr Hyde! A pleasure! *(Pause)* Boys' night out?

HYDE: My date's at the bar.

HOLLYWOOD: I saw her. *(Pause)* How's your new picture coming?

HYDE: Back on track now. We start shooting in a couple of weeks.

HOLLYWOOD: It's about a business tycoon, isn't it?

HYDE: How did you — ? We've been trying different occupations for the main character....

HOLLYWOOD: I always wondered, how did you manage to breathe such life into your portrayal of Napoleon?

HYDE: I studied him, Mr Confidential. I studied him very carefully.

HOLLYWOOD: I suppose you've always had a fascination for the darker personality.

HYDE: I'd call it the mad, the jealous, the power-hungry.

HOLLYWOOD: Well, I look forward to it. By the way, there's another friend of yours in the Florentine Room who seems to be having some trouble holding his liquor. You might want to see he gets home okay before he collapses. Nice to see you again, Mr Hyde....

(HOLLYWOOD *exits or moves off.* HYDE *and* DAVID *watch him.*)

HYDE: You didn't tell me he was here!

DAVID: What did you expect?

HYDE: Have you read what he's been saying about me?

DAVID: Of course.

(Pause)

HYDE: Where did Hollywood Confidential come from, anyway?

DAVID: What do you mean?

HYDE: Who *is* he?

DAVID: Eddie Harrell found him, probably hacking away at some rewrite desk, and put him on gossip because he knew so much about the pictures. He's sharp as a whip, you know. Clearly started out wanting to be in the business himself.

HYDE: People like that. Who have no real gifts of their own....

DAVID: Oh, they've got real gifts, alright. It's just that those gifts were given to them by a different God.

(Pause. Laughter from off-stage.)

DAVID: There's Roz. Man your battle stations.

HYDE: It's something else, isn't it.

DAVID: What?

HYDE: Your suggesting I get married.

DAVID: Of course not. *(Pause)* Like what?

HYDE: I don't know. Like maybe you don't love me anymore.

ACT ONE

DAVID: But that's just it. How could I not love you? You're impossible. Self-centered, egotistical, depraved. Everything I look for in a man. You're also famous, a part of you I could easily do without.

HYDE: Would you risk it? If I moved back?

DAVID: Of course. But how...

HYDE: I don't know how to fight what I think is going on. And I have a feeling it's going to get worse. I...I'm nothing without my work. I have to make my picture.

DAVID: Then for God's sake, make it! Do whatever it takes and GET IT DONE! Because without it, you're no good to either of us.

(Pause)

HYDE: By the way, thanks for the freesia.

DAVID: The freesia?

HYDE: For my birthday. I thought the boy was a bit much, and not really your style, but amusing, all the same....

DAVID: I didn't send you any freesia for your birthday.

HYDE: You didn't?

DAVID: No. And *who* was the boy?

(REYNALDO ROMERO enters in a tight state, rather stonily drunk and upset. He goes to them.)

REYNALDO: Julian... Excuse please...forgive me....

HYDE: Reynaldo, are you all right?

REYNALDO: Please...I hope you can find it in your heart to...forgive me.

HYDE: What is it? What's happened?

REYNALDO: I didn't mean to tell him...all the things.... I even thought, when he see me, I thought he even *likes* me....

HYDE: *(Darkly)* Reynaldo... What are you talking about? Tell what to whom?

REYNALDO: But he cannot print.... He promise me, he will not print....

HYDE: Hollywood Confidential...? You talked to Hollywood Confidential...?

REYNALDO: What could I do? Mr Hock and Bernie Bugle...they say they will fire me anyway! They do! They tell me that! In spite of what you tell them!

(HYDE *becomes very frightened and angry. He shakes* REYNALDO.)

HYDE: What did you tell him? He asked you to tell him about me? About David and me? WHAT DID YOU TELL HIM?! YOU BASTARD! WHAT?

(He shakes REYNALDO. REYNALDO *weeps.)*

REYNALDO: Tomorrow...my career will be over.... Forgive me...

(He rushes off.)

HYDE: Reynaldo! Come back here! Reynaldo!

(DAVID *has restrained* HYDE. HYDE, *embarrassed at hitting* REYNALDO, *shakes, upset.)*

HYDE: I'm sorry.... I didn't mean to.... I don't know what came over me....

DAVID: He was in love with you. Don't you understand? He was in love with you....

(From offstage, a shot is fired. The club quiets. HYDE *straightens up.)*

HYDE: My God...

ACT ONE 43

DAVID: You should get out of here. The police are going to be here any minute.

HYDE: Jesus... But... Reynaldo...

DAVID: I'LL TAKE CARE OF IT! JUST GET OUT OF HERE!

(He drags HYDE *by the arm, and they exit as shouts and cries are heard.* REYNALDO *reenters, holding his head, followed by* SUGIE.)

REYNALDO: A failure! I try to shoot myself, and I cannot even do that!

SUGIE: Everybody calm down.... It was an accident.... Somebody call a doctor.... All of you, go back to enjoying yourselves.... Dave the Beachcomber! Let's rhumba!

(Music starts up as lights go down on the Club Conga and come up on HOCK's *office.* HOCK *alone, onstage. Intercom buzzes.)*

VOICE: Mr Hyde is here, Mr Hock.

HOCK: Send him in.

(Pause. HYDE *enters.)*

HYDE: Hiya, Charley. Singer and I should have a completed script within the week. That only means delaying shooting by about a few days...and the budget problems have been resolved....

HOCK: Sit down, Julian.

HYDE: Also, you're going to love what we've come up with for an opening....

HOCK: There's not going to be an opening just yet....

HYDE: I know, I know, you'll want to fight with me about changing it....

HOCK: There's not going to be a beginning or a middle, either....

HYDE: Of course there is.

HOCK: No. I'm sorry. Because at the moment, there may not be a picture.

HYDE: What...?

(Pause)

HOCK: Hollywood Confidential telephoned me this morning. He knows, Julian. He knows about you and your friendship with David Hogarth during the time you were married to Lida. He's threatening to go public with it.

HYDE: What? Go public? But he can't!

HOCK: I don't think he can, either — but he can make life very difficult for us — for you, me, and this Studio....

HYDE: *(To self)* Why is he doing this...?

HOCK: Now, I've begged him — convinced him to hold off. He's agreed on one condition — that he come over here and make a deal with you.

HYDE: A deal? What kind of deal?

HOCK: He wouldn't say.

HYDE: Jesus Christ... What...what is going on?

HOCK: People are scared.

HYDE: But that's why he must be stopped. If he isn't stopped now, there's no telling where this will end! Look, you've known about me, what I was, what I am, all along — but what mattered was the talent — and the pictures! Or have you suddenly forgotten them?

HOCK: Of course I haven't. But times have changed.

ACT ONE

HYDE: And what am I supposed to do? Change along with them?

HOCK: No! You're supposed to stay exactly as you are!

HYDE: But what I am is not what I seem! You must understand — you're a Jew also —

HOCK: I'm not a Jew! I'm an American! There's a difference, do you understand? And you — you don't even look like a Jew, which is why you've had such a successful career!

(HYDE *starts to laugh.*)

HYDE: I don't look like a Jew, so maybe I'm not a Jew?... Do I look like a pansy?

HOCK: Don't call yourself that!

HYDE: Why not?! Charley, that's what I am!

HOCK: Why couldn't you have done like I'd asked and gone to some German headshrinker and had this disease of yours, this sickness, routed out of you? There are things they do with chemicals, with injections, with electricity....

HYDE: Why not removal of that part of the brain entirely! Complete brain transference! We could make a picture about it, Charley, *The Sexually Inverted Frankenstein*....

(HYDE *laughs, a bit hysterically.*)

HOCK: Stop making jokes!

HYDE: Stop insulting me!

HOCK: I want you to make this picture, you understand?

HYDE: Of course!

HOCK: Then whatever deal he wants to make, I suggest you make it.

(Pause. Intercom buzzes.)

VOICE: Hollywood Confidential is here, Mr Hock.

HOCK: Send him in.

(Pause. HOLLYWOOD CONFIDENTIAL *enters.* HYDE *stares at him.)*

HOCK: HC! How are you!

HOLLYWOOD: Very well, Charley, couldn't be better! Loved *Follies and Frolics*. That was some swell preview....

HOCK: It did seem to wow 'em, didn't it....

HOLLYWOOD: This Patsy Morgan could be another Jeannette MacDonald! At least, that's what I'm going to say in my column tomorrow!

HOCK: Why, thanks, she sure could use it! *(Pause)* You know Julian Hyde, don't you?

HOLLYWOOD: Yes, of course.

HOCK: If you gentlemen will excuse me, I have some business to attend to....

HOLLYWOOD: We're not throwing you out of your office, are we?

HOCK: Not at all. I've got to see the studio doc for my annual, you know....

HOLLYWOOD: Had quite a few of those annuals recently, haven't you?

*(*HOCK *looks surprised and upset.)*

HOCK: Why, no, as a matter of... *(Laughs)* When you get to be my age....

HOLLYWOOD: Of course, of course, an age I'm sure I'll never reach....

ACT ONE

HOCK: I hope, for your sake, you don't! I'll call you later, Julian. Remember what we talked about....

(HOCK *leaves the room.*)

HOLLYWOOD: A very good man, Charley Hock. Done a lot for the picture business.

HYDE: More than you know.

HOLLYWOOD: Too bad his time at Hock Studios may soon be coming to an end....

HYDE: I beg your pardon?

HOLLYWOOD: I shouldn't be telling tales out of school. But it's a curse, my profession. Makes me a habitual snitch...

HYDE: *(Evenly)* What about Charley?

HOLLYWOOD: Well, like he admitted...he's not in the best of health. The word is, according to his doctor....

(Pause)

HYDE: Jesus...

HOLLYWOOD: I'm afraid some of the the members of the Board of Hock International haven't been very happy with Charley's most recent pictures. *Follies and Frolics* indeed! Quite frankly, they're counting on you to make a real winner. Otherwise, a gentle push in the direction of Uncle Charley's failing health might just shake things up a bit....

HYDE: Who on the board?

HOLLYWOOD: Now that would be telling....

HYDE: Is this your way of making sure I agree to do whatever you want?

HOLLYWOOD: If there's one thing I know about you, Julian, it's that movies mean more to you than life itself.

HYDE: And what means so much to you?

HOLLYWOOD: My readers.

HYDE: Oh, yes. Your readers. Those seekers of the truth. Your readers and my audience. We are both slaves to them, aren't we?

HOLLYWOOD: Apparently not. You seem to have betrayed your fans. They've given you their love, and what have you done with it? Spat on it. Degraded them by degrading yourself...

HYDE: My fans and my life have nothing to do with each other....

HOLLYWOOD: No? And what was Lida Todd if not a fan who became part of your life?! And you degraded HER.... And ruined her life!

HYDE: Oh, how dramatic! How very like the headlines you scream out at your readers day after day! Today JULIAN HYDE RUINED LIDA'S LIFE! And what will your headlines scream out tomorrow, Mr Confidential?

HOLLYWOOD: Just this: Pretty Boy Reynaldo Romero Dead from a Second Suicide Attempt.

(Pause. HYDE reacts to this news as if hit in the stomach. When he speaks again, it is as if from deep inside himself.)

HOLLYWOOD: You... You knew him, didn't you, Mr Hyde?

HYDE: Yes...I...

HOLLYWOOD: As a matter of fact, if I'm not mistaken, didn't you have an argument with him after I left the Conga Club the other night?

HYDE: You seem to know quite a lot, Mr Confidential. What else do you know...?

ACT ONE 49

HOLLYWOOD: Oh, all sorts of interesting things. For instance... doesn't freesia happen to be your favorite flower?

(Pause)

HYDE: What...what do you want from me?

HOLLYWOOD: Publicists are paid to keep scoops away from people like me, Mr Hyde. That's their job. I want somebody to help me outdo Hedda, Louella, Winchell, and all the other gossips on both coasts combined. Since your Mr Hogarth is a publicist at a major studio, he knows all the personal and political affiliations of his stars.... And surely, much of this information he tells you...or you could easily find out....

HYDE: You want David...to spy?

HOLLYWOOD: No, Mr Hyde...I want *you*...to spy on David.... *(Pause)* I think you should move back in with him. It's what you want, isn't it? I know it's what David wants. Why not call him and find out?

(He offers HYDE *the telephone. Pause.* HYDE *slowly dials.)*

HYDE: David Hogarth, please... Hello? David?... It's Julian.... What?... No, I'm fine.... I've been thinking about things, and.... I think we should risk it.... You know what.... No, I think we should.... Don't worry... It'll be okay.... I've worked things out.... I'll — I'll explain when I see you.... Yes... And, David?... I love you.... Bye...

*(*HYDE *hangs up.* HYDE *turns away, his mind suddenly thinking and racing.)*

HOLLYWOOD: That wasn't so tough, was it?

HYDE: No... Not so tough... Not so tough at all...

HOLLYWOOD: Then you'll do it...?

HYDE: Do it? Yes... Yes, I'll do it... Because I know now, for the first time, I really know...what else I must do....

(*Lights fade on* HOCK's *office now and concentrate on* HYDE *and* HOLLYWOOD *solely. As* HYDE *speaks, the stage becomes filled with lights, cameras, and a* FILM CREW, *and* HYDE *becomes transformed, by putting on a costume and having coat, hat, etc. placed on him, into a duplicate of* HOLLYWOOD CONFIDENTIAL. HYDE *and* HOLLYWOOD *speak simultaneously.*)

HOLLYWOOD: Who do you want to know about? Who? Who do you want to know about? Who? Who? Lana Turner? Joan Crawford? Douglas Fairbanks? How about Mary Pickford? Who did Jean Harlow spend the night with? What happened to Paul Bern? Who shot William Desmond Taylor? What about Clark? And Carole? And Claudette? And Dick? Who do you want to know about? Who? Who? WHO?

HYDE: I will make a picture that will stop this man, this evil.... I am going to make sure that Hollywood Confidential never gets to say terrible things about anybody ever again.... But to do that I first have to try and understand him.... Who is he? Where did he come from? What makes him the way he is?... And why is he attacking me so much? Why me?

VOICE 1: Are we ready?

VOICE 2: Ready!

HYDE: I will fight him with the greatest power of light that I have....

VOICE 3: Lights!

VOICE 2: Roll 'em!

HYDE: ...With my picture! MY PICTURE WILL DESTROY MY ENEMY...!

ACT ONE

(HYDE, *transformed, has become* HOLLYWOOD CONFIDENTIAL. *The real* HOLLYWOOD *disappears.* HYDE *turns and extends his arms, possessing the stage, staring out at us, as we hear:*)

VOICE: Action!

(Lights shine bright on HYDE *and the curtain quickly falls.)*

END ACT ONE

ACT TWO

(Lights rise on HARRY BABYLON *in a spotlight.* HARRY *is a newspaper columnist who looks and sounds like* HOLLYWOOD CONFIDENTIAL. *He is played by* JULIAN HYDE.*)*

BABYLON: I'm in this room. It's a big place, very classy, almost posh. Lots of red velvet and chandeliers hanging from the ceilings. I don't know if it's New York or L.A., but it feels like L.A.... Seems to be some kind of picture premiere, 'cause there's lots of celebs. I look over and see Lolly Parsons, and I think, Christ, whoever is here, she's gonna scoop me. And sure enough, when I turn back, I see Kate Hepburn walking towards her. Only it isn't really Kate, 'cause she's wearing the same splashy gown Lola Lane wore in *Hollywood Hotel,* and Hepburn wouldn't be caught dead wearing anything like that. But she's got Kate's laugh, so I think maybe it's somebody pretending to *be* Kate, only Lola Lane's gown was the only thing she could find to wear. Or maybe it's Kate pretending to be Lola Lane. But why would Kate Hepburn want to do something crazy like that? Besides, what's Lola Lane wearing, if Kate Hepburn's got her gown? And where *is* Lola Lane, anyway? *(Pause)* Then I look around and realize things are a little screwy everywhere. For example, Cary Grant is standing at the bar talking to Virginia Mayo, but he's wearing Franchot Tone's Indian getup from *Lives of a Bengal Lancer.* And Franchot Tone is sitting under a potted palm, talking to nobody in particular in a voice that sounds like W. C. Fields. Deanna Durbin's at the piano, singing *My Bill* to Helen Morgan, who's dressed like Hattie MacDaniel in *Gone With The Wind.* It's crazy, it's all crazy, I gotta get out of here, I think to myself, and just as I do, I turn and see Gary Cooper, the Coop, coming towards me, and I feel like rushing into his arms and bawling like a baby. *(Pause)* "Hi, Coop, how are ya?" I say to him. "I'm fine, Harry, I couldn't be better," he says right back. Only, there's something funny about his voice. It sounds familiar, but it doesn't sound like him. "Care for a dwink, dahling?" he says. And then I realize. Dietrich. It's Gary Cooper, but he's got Marlene Dietrich's voice, and before I know it, he starts humming *Falling In Love Again* and pawing at me like I'm Emil Jannings in *The Blue Angel.* "Get off me, get away from me," I cry, but the Coop doesn't seem to hear, 'cause his painted fingernails are crawling up my neck now, and there's a slit up his pant leg a mile long and it flashes black silk stockings and high heels. I sock him in the tits and turn away, but everybody's laughing at me, everybody's grabbing, I see Cary Grant cracking his whip and Adolphe Menjou made up like Rita Hayworth, and they're all laughing, laughing, laughing at me. "I helped create you, I created all of you — stop it," I shout, "Stop it, STOP IT YOU MONSTERS, STOP IT!" And I run to the door, but it's locked, and they're all after me now, following me like I'm Olga Baclanova and they're the freaks in *Freaks* and before I know it they're on me, pulling and tugging and ripping and eating, their teeth tearing into me, their jaws making candy out of my flesh. "I'm sorry!" I cry, "I'm sorry for everything, for everything I ever did or said about any of you, I'm sorry I'M SORRY I'M SORRY!" *(Pause)* And when I wake up, I'm nowhere. I'm nothing. I'm not anything.

ACT TWO 55

There are pieces of me in Roz and Cary and Coop and Tallulah. There's an eyeball, and der Bingle's got it. There's a toenail, and it's on the Duke's big toe. There's my tongue in Bette Davis' purse, and an earlobe next to Kate's Oscar. I'm spread out all over Hollywood, and I'm not anything anymore. Nothing but the wind. There's a hint of me on Harlow's breath...but...otherwise...I'm gone....

(Spotlight widens around BABYLON *to include a night club looking like a movie version of the Club Conga — only a small slice of it, perhaps.* BABYLON *enters and is pursued and accosted by various picture people.)*

PRESS AGENT: Evening, Harry!

BABYLON: Hiya, Nate! What have you got for me?

PRESS AGENT: Cary sure would appreciate it if you put in something about his latest picture.

BABYLON: What about his latest divorce?

PRESS AGENT: I'd lie low on that, if you don't mind.

BABYLON: Mind? Of course I mind! You think my readers just want to know that Cary's made another picture? Of course not! They want to know why the heck he can't keep a woman!

*(*SENATOR PENNY *approaches* BABYLON.*)*

SENATOR: Evening, Harry! Sorry if this is a bad time — we won't stay too long — don't want to wear out our welcome —

BABYLON: Not at all, Senator. Always a pleasure. That was some lovely-looking lady I saw you with at the races the other day. A friend of Mrs Penny's?

SENATOR: Er — no, not exactly.

BABYLON: I'm sure your wife would just love to read about her in my column tomorrow.

SENATOR: Now, hold on, Harry — what do you want from me?

BABYLON: What can you tell me about that young lawyer your party's putting up for congressional election next year? What is he, a lawyer?

SENATOR: Law professor, Harry.

BABYLON: Oh, I get it. Wouldn't be surprised if he was a little Red around the gills....

SENATOR: Oh, I don't think — well — definitely has — maybe some Reddish tendencies....

BABYLON: My readers don't like politics much, Joe. But they like lawyers even less. I'd like you to get some loyalty information on him that I could use....

(An AGENT approaches BABYLON with an ACTRESS.)

AGENT: Hiya, Harry, I want you to meet a wonderful new talent....

BABYLON: What makes you think I'm talking to you this month, Fred?

AGENT: What? But Harry, I just want you to say hello to....

BABYLON: I'm still sore at you for icing me out of the Gable-Lombard wedding.

AGENT: I didn't ice you out! I tried finding you all day! Besides, Clark had cold feet up until the last moment. We thought he'd hightailed it to Cuba and was never coming back....

BABYLON: *(To* ACTRESS*)* You like this man?

ACTRESS: Why, yes, Mr Babylon...

BABYLON: I'd advise you against signing with him. Call Buddy Driver, he handles Lana, and I'll put in a good word for you.

ACT TWO

ACTRESS: How do you know I'm worth it, Mr Babylon?

BABYLON: Simple. Buddy here is a great judge of talent.

ACTRESS: Then why wouldn't I want to sign with him?

BABYLON: *(To* AGENT*)* A bright girl. *(To* ACTRESS*)* Ours is not to reason why, my dear. We are born into this world, and must make of it and ourselves what we can. Talented people must create, but they mustn't be indulged. Their lives are mirrors against which the unhappy public can dream. *(Pause)* If you want me to help you, you're going to have to find another manager. Otherwise, no dice.

ACTRESS: Thank you, Mr Babylon. *(Exits)*

AGENT: Sylvia! Wait!

BABYLON: Next time tell me about the wedding bells BEFORE they ring.

(AGENT *moves off. A young Latin lover-type actor enters and goes to* BABYLON's *table.*)

RICARDO: Excuse me, Mr Babylon...I am most desperate.... My manager warn me not to come here.... But I must talk with you....

BABYLON: I have nothing to say to you, Mr Milan.

RICARDO: What you write about me.... I have never dated a girl who is a Communiste, Mr Babylon....

BABYLON: That poetess attended meetings at the home of Salka Viertel....

RICARDO: But she not know what papers she sign! Please, I have told her she must never see those people again....

BABYLON: I don't want you to see her anymore, Ricardo.

RICARDO: But...but I love this girl.... We are engaged to be married....

BABYLON: Then un-engage yourself... Or stop making pictures...

(RICARDO *starts to cry.* BABYLON *grows excited. He starts to shake him.*)

BABYLON: Stop it. Stop crying. You're soft. Just like a woman. Stop it! You're weak, do you understand? If you were any sort of man you'd stop this grovelling! Fight me! Hit me! KILL ME! But I hate your petty little snivelling....

RICARDO: I will kill you, if I have to.... I SWEAR, I WILL!

BABYLON: You can't kill me! You don't have it in you.... You...may as well kill yourself.... *(He suddenly stops.)* No, no, no... Christ!

VOICE: Where are we?

VOICE #2: What is he doing?

BABYLON: ...Can we just stop...? Please...?

VOICE: CUT!

(Immediately lights come up full.)

VOICE: How was that?

VOICE #2: That looked dandy.

VOICE #3: Sound was okey-dokey.

ANDREW: Julian?

HYDE: I hated it. *(Pause)* I'm sorry, I.... It just isn't feeling right....

ANDREW: The bit with Ricardo? Or the entire —

HYDE: The whole scene! I'm just not getting it!

(Pause)

ANDREW: It looked fine to me....

HYDE: Fine? It can't just be fine! It needs to be a lot more than fine!

RICARDO: Is there something I can....

HYDE: No! No... It isn't you.... It's me....

(Pause)

ANDREW: Well... Should we do it again?

HYDE: Yes, yes... Of course... Again and again and again...

(Silence)

RICARDO: Do we have to do the part where you shake me?

ANDREW: Yes, we'll need that shake....

HYDE: Where is Susan? There's a problem with Miss Fenmore's hair.

SUSAN: Sir?

HYDE: It shouldn't be pulled back.

SUSAN: We tried keeping it loose, but it blocks her face in that light....

HYDE: Then we need to re-mark her.

ACTRESS: Mr Hyde, I really don't like letting my hair just fall —

HYDE: It has to! That's the way I want it! Lida's hair was always loose....

SUSAN: I beg your pardon?

HYDE: I want that hair left untied. It makes her look more innocent. Less severe. The severity comes from within. Can you be more severe from within, Miss Fenmore?

ACTRESS: I — I can certainly try.

HYDE: Good. *(Calls)* Where is Perry? I don't think the lights on the tables should be so bright.

ART DIRECTOR: We tried dimming them before, Julian, remember? It causes too much shadow around you and Ricardo.

HYDE: Start the lights bright as the crane shot moves over the restaurant. Then dim them as we move in for the close-up.

ART DIRECTOR: That'll take another half-hour to re-adjust.

HYDE: *(Calls)* Where is Jake? Jake?!

(JAKE *appears from the side of the stage.*)

HYDE: How did that look to you?

JAKE: You've done at least fifteen takes on this scene, and the first one looked as good as the last....

HYDE: I think Babylon is becoming too sympathetic in it.

JAKE: Too sympathetic?

HYDE: I know he's flesh and blood, after all, not some apparition I've dreamt up in my head. But I don't want the audience to care, maybe not at all until....

ANDREW: Mr Hyde? I'm sorry, but er Mr Hock....

HYDE: Yes? What about him?

ANDREW: He just called to say that...well...he's sending somebody down to the set.

HYDE: What do you mean, sending somebody down? Nobody's allowed on the set unless I approve them, you know that....

ANDREW: Yes, but, Mr Hock wants us to move on....

ACT TWO

HYDE: Oh, he does, does he?

ANDREW: Well, since we're already ten days behind....

HYDE: Behind, yes...ten days, as I am told every day, at the end of every day....

ANDREW: We still have several hours if....

HYDE: If we want to forget about the take and just move on??

ANDREW: The first take was quite excellent, as Mr Singer suggested....

HYDE: Mr Singer is only the writer, Andrew. He isn't directing this picture, or starring in it, to my knowledge.

ANDREW: Yes, Sir. But Mr Hock also suggests that there are such things as close-ups to break up a scene of this kind....

HYDE: A scene of this kind? What does Mr Hock know about a scene of this kind?? Doesn't Mr Hock realize that I am shooting this picture in continuity and cutting it with the camera? That should reduce considerably the number of angles, Andrew, wouldn't you say?

ANDREW: Yessir, but, Mr Hock kindly submits that eliminating additional angles without eliminating the time that is spent on these additional angles...doesn't really...eliminate...anything....

HYDE: Would Mr Hock like to direct this picture?

ANDREW: I don't think....

HYDE: Or maybe you would like to direct it? Would you like to take over from here?

ANDREW: Why, no, Sir, I...

HYDE: You mean you refuse?

ANDREW: No, of course not, but...

HYDE: Then direct, Andrew, with my blessing, and call me when we're back on schedule!

ANDREW: Sir, this is so... *(As* HYDE *leaves the set)* unlike you....

(Pause. JAKE *starts to follow* HYDE *out, passing* ANDREW *as he does.)*

JAKE: I'll talk to him.

ANDREW: Please, Mr Singer. He's been...impossible lately....

JAKE: It's alright. Set up for the newspaper office.

ANDREW: But what about—are we going to have to reshoot?

*(*JAKE *shrugs as if to say "Who knows?" He pats* ANDREW *on the back and exits after* HYDE. *Pause.)*

VOICE #3: Are we going on?

ANDREW: Yes. Yes. We're going on....

(The set begins to fracture as people and voices are seen and heard coming from everywhere.)

VOICE #4: Sound?

VOICE #5: Do we have continuity?

VOICE #3: We're okey-dokey.

ANDREW: Newspaper office. We are going on to the newspaper office....

*(*ANDREW *exits and the set fractures and disappears as lights come up on* JAKE *and* HYDE *in his dressing room.)*

HYDE: Hock this! Hock that! What does he expect of me?! What do they all expect of me?! "You've averaged only two script pages a day, Mr Hyde".... "You've only done ten camera setups today, Sir"....

ACT TWO

"The front office says you took twenty-four minutes to light three setups each yesterday...." Do they really think I can possibly go any faster?!

JAKE: You always have these fights with them, Julian....

HYDE: Yes, but not like this! Never like this!

JAKE: Yeah, but you've never made so many changes — including the entire goddamn story — on a picture before!

HYDE: They should trust me! I'm worth my reputation!

JAKE: Of course you are! But you also happen to be complaining about your acting more than ever!

HYDE: I know when I'm good and when I'm not. It's as simple as that. I must be — I have to get it absolutely right.... *(Pause)* Remind me to talk to Wally Westmore. This makeup is becoming unbearable under those lights.... *(Pause)* Did you get to the girl back home?

JAKE: Sophie Hotchkiss. Daughter of the local judge. Cheerleader at Chappawick High School. He got her knocked up. Scarlet Letter time. Must have seen his bright and shining future disappearing before him. He ran away from home. The baby was born premature and died shortly after birth.

HYDE: We might be able to use that. In the flashback sequence...

JAKE: I already have....

(He hands HYDE *pages.* HYDE *looks over them intently.)*

JAKE: There's something else....

HYDE: *(Reading)* Good, Jake, these are very good....

JAKE: The stuff he's been telling folks on the air — about his picture-perfect all-American boyhood. It's all made up. His Dad was a furniture salesman who stole some money from his boss and left town before Herman was born.

HYDE: Is his mom still in that institution?

JAKE: *(Nods)* Herman lived with different foster families for five or six years. Two of them wouldn't talk to us, the third's moved out of state. One foster father, Clarence Darwood, used to beat him, or so Herman once told a friend.

HYDE: Did you contact the man?

JAKE: Not yet.

HYDE: Well, what are you waiting for?! I want you to talk to every member of that family — also, have you found out any more about that girlfriend of his?

JAKE: He did meet her after he started working for Eddie Harrell. She was going around trying to get work at the Studios, and he went along with her. They were practically engaged when she left him.

HYDE: She left him?

JAKE: Well, they broke up. His old landlady said he never quite quite seemed the same after that.

HYDE: And the girl?

JAKE: She only saw her a few times, said she didn't know her name. Most of the folks who knew him don't want to talk about him. Afraid, probably.

HYDE: I can just guess why. Find out who the girl was, and if she's still living here in Los Angeles.

JAKE: Julian, I'm sorry, but I can't.

HYDE: Can't?! What are you talking about?

ACT TWO

JAKE: I want you to take me off this picture.

HYDE: What...?! Are you joking?

JAKE: Please.

HYDE: Of course not! I'm still shooting, aren't I? I told you, I need an ending! How is this picture going to end?!

JAKE: How should I know?! That's been your indecision all along, not mine!

HYDE: Are you abandoning me?

JAKE: Don't put it like that!

HYDE: How else should I put it? I need you!

JAKE: I know that, but right now, I need me more! I'm going back to New York, Julian.

HYDE: What?!

JAKE: You heard me. I'm getting the hell out of here and going back. All the way back, if I can help it — to the Williamsburg section of Brooklyn —

HYDE: You've gone crazy, haven't you?

JAKE: I've never been more sane. I've started work on a new play.

(HYDE *bursts out laughing.*)

JAKE: What's so funny? Don't you believe me?

HYDE: A play? That's a good one!

JAKE: I have!

HYDE: You wouldn't know what a play was if it jumped up and socked you in the face! When was the last time you typed "The curtain rises" without being soaked in gin?

JAKE: Just last week! And I intend to keep writing that way until I type "The curtain falls"! I'm getting out, do you understand? I've had it with this lousy place! Stalin's signed with Hitler, and England's gone to war, and there's too much going on in the world for me to worry about Andy Hardy's latest loves! Let them get some other hack to write his dialogue! I've got bigger stuff on my mind....

HYDE: And this isn't big? What we're doing? For God's sake, his new radio show has become number one in the country!

JAKE: Believe me, I know! I listen to it every week! I have to — my director has become his biggest fan!

HYDE: It's Marian, isn't it? You've made it up, and now you're going back to her —

JAKE: No, for God's sake, we're dead, and all I care about is my son! Martin's who I want to go back and see!

HYDE: He's four years old! Wait till he's all grown up.

JAKE: I also have a career to think about, Julian.

HYDE: And who can you thank for it?! Who can you thank for everything in your career? Ungrateful! You're all so ungrateful!

JAKE: I am not ungrateful! I've worked very hard for you, pally. You can use that on your actors, but you can't use it on me....

HYDE: You know the way I work!

JAKE: Yes, I know — you're like a vortex — whirling, obsessed, sucking everything around you into yourself! It may be exciting, but it isn't always pleasant. Or productive! *(Pause)* Look, when you started making changes in this picture, and told me who it'd be about — well, I worked as hard as I could.... We've got more than enough material on

ACT TWO

him, and I don't see why we just can't finalize the script and—

HYDE: BECAUSE I NEED TO KNOW EVERYTHING ABOUT HIM! EVERYTHING!

JAKE: Why? So you can portray him? Or destroy him?

HYDE: Both!

(Pause)

JAKE: It's poisoning me, writing this picture. And it's poisoning you, too. Since I started writing about Harry Babylon's rise and fall, I've begun to really question why I do what I do. Much as I despise our Mr Confidential, I keep wondering, could my little pen make such a difference in the way others see him? If I do the same thing to him that he's been doing to everybody else, will I still be able to live with myself? Of course, I'm just the writer. It's your picture. But you can't fight him, Julian. If you spend all your time fighting him, you'll become just like him yourself.

HYDE: Look at me, Jake... Who am I...? *(Pause)* I have to pass through him to get to the other side.

JAKE: Just don't lose yourself along the way.

HYDE: Stay with me. Help me finish this. There is a war on. More than one.

JAKE: I know. The world is already a very frightening place.

HYDE: For us, especially. Two Jews.

JAKE: And one Red.

HYDE: And one fairy. Four of the worst of everything...

(Pause)

JAKE: I wonder where we'll all be in another three years....

(Pause. A shadowy figure appears, hesitates, enters. It is the FLORIST.*)*

HYDE: Perhaps our friend the gentle Aryan knows the answer to that....

JAKE: See you tomorrow.

*(*JAKE *leaves.* HYDE *turns to the* FLORIST.*)*

HYDE: And how are you today, my blonde beauty? No freesia to deliver? But you need an inscription, don't you? Let's see. *(He writes out a card.)* "Clark Gable insisted Cukor be fired from *Gone With the Wind* because Cukor knew of Gable's early days as a gigolo.... Comedy director L. M. sympathetic to German cause... Charles Laughton arrested on morals charge, but young man quietly paid off...."

(Pause. He hands it back to FLORIST.*)*

HYDE: With love, from Louis B. Mayer... I trust the thought will please. *(Pause)* Are you proud of yourself, young man? Is this what you thought being a member of your pleasure-giving profession would be like?

FLORIST: I know you won't believe this, Sir, but...I happen to be a big fan of yours....

HYDE: Oh, I believe it, my boy. You certainly seemed to enjoy our little tour of the set....

FLORIST: I love going to the pictures.

HYDE: Yes. But do you think they can actually change things?

FLORIST: I — I don't know, Sir.

HYDE: No. Neither do I....

*(*FLORIST *leaves.* HYDE *watches him go. He turns back, his face a mask. He stands alone for several seconds.)*

ACT TWO

HYDE: "I have a little shadow, it goes in and out with me.... And what can be the use of him...is more than I can see...."

(Pause. Slowly, deliberately, HYDE *goes to the radio. Turns it on.)*

ANNOUNCER: And now, The Lux Ledger, featuring Hollywood Confidential...

HOLLYWOOD: Good evening, Mr and Mrs America, and all our friends overseas...

(Lights go down on HYDE *as a spot comes up on* HOLLYWOOD CONFIDENTIAL *in front of a microphone, on the radio. He speaks rapidly, with great self-importance, punctuating his news items with telegraph flashes that he operates himself.)*

HOLLYWOOD: I've just been on the phone with the President, who promises me he will do all he can to prevent us from having to fight the Devil Hun, Adolph, that screaming swastika the King Ratzi himself. So let's light a candle for Queen Victoria, Mom, and pray for our Allies in their great cause.... Senator Tenney now admits that the Hollywood community is rife with members of the Communist Party, and is calling for a complete investigation. No fooling, Ma and Pa, your homes, your livelihood, the very safety of your children may be threatened.... And did you know that movie mogul Harry Cohn's office has been remodelled to resemble Mussolini's? Somebody should tell Mr Cohn he's supporting the wrong side. Mamamia, Harry, read up on your politics.... Boy, would I love to tell you some juicy tidbits about Clark Gable's past! But don't ask me, ask a picture director whose initials are Gable's, reversed... Movie star director genius Julian Hyde is apparently having tremendous trouble on his latest picture, now retitled *Harry Babylon: His Rise and Fall*....

Insiders say he's changed the storyline and it's now about a gossip columnist. Friends of the director say he doesn't even have an ending yet! He's been going crazy and is now almost three weeks behind! Studio head Charles Hock is threatening to close the entire picture down. Forget about Harry Babylon! Could this be the fall of Julian Hyde?... What Henry Luce editor is so scared he wants to cancel the romance with the wife he thefted from a famous congressman, and stay home with his own?... Back in a jiffy...

(HOLLYWOOD *turns off the mike as* ANNOUNCER *is heard selling Lux Liquid.* HOLLYWOOD, *in a rage, calls out quickly:*)

HOLLYWOOD: Betty! Betty!

(BETTY *appears and goes to him.*)

HOLLYWOOD: What the hell is this?

BETTY: What's the matter?

HOLLYWOOD: There's another item here on Senator Tenney! Don't you edit these goddamn things?

BETTY: Of course I do! But one must have gotten past me!

HOLLYWOOD: No more on Tenney this month!

BETTY: Right!

AUDIO MAN: Five seconds, Hollywood...

HOLLYWOOD: He's a fat slob, anyway....

ANNOUNCER: And now back to the Lux Ledger, featuring Hollywood Confidential....

HOLLYWOOD: My final note tonight is a message of thanks for the great support all of you listeners have given us in our drive to stamp out sin and sinfulness in this great nation... Back in my hometown of Chappawick, my Daddy used to tell me, just 'cause a man calls you by your first name doesn't mean he's your friend. I think you folks know what I'm talking about. Why is it that we poor struggling fools, you and me, never see ourselves depicted in those Hollywood movies? Why are we always watching fancy people living in fancy houses attended to by fancy butlers who are prissy to boot? I'll tell you why. Because those are the types of folks who live in Hollywood, and they don't care about the common man. There are stars living together out of wedlock, having babies and abortions directly in the face of God. There are starlets with severe emotional and sexual problems who have to see headshrinkers to try and cure their sick ways. There are more divorces going on in Beverly Hills than there are in any other city in the union. And what effect does all this ungodly behavior have on the pictures you and your loved ones enjoy watching at your local picture palace? We shudder to think. Remember, when you see a scene depicted in your movie theater that offends your honor as an American, or corrupts the mind of your favorite son or daughter, write to your senator or congressman, or call me, Hollywood Confidential, and I'll do my best to get an apology from Louis B Mayer, himself. So, good night, Shirley Temple, wherever you are, and with Lux of Love, I remain your Hollywood correspondent, Hollywood Confidential....

(He turns off. ANNOUNCER *is heard finishing the broadcast as* HOLLYWOOD *immediately starts talking.)*

HOLLYWOOD: Are there calls coming in?

AUDIO MAN: Phone's already ringing.

HOLLYWOOD: Good, good!

BETTY: You're going to get a lot of heat from Mayer about that Gable wisecrack....

HOLLYWOOD: What do I care?!

BETTY: The Studio heads are getting very upset....

HOLLYWOOD: The President was listening again tonight, did you know that? He's quite a little hypocrite! He tells Senators and Congressmen he's unhappy with my political meddling, but when I met him last week, he wanted to know all my dirty jokes! And he asked me if I knew anything about J. Edgar Hoover's sex life! Imagine! The President asking me!

AUDIO MAN: You just got a call from Nita Naldi.

HOLLYWOOD: Who the hell is that?

AUDIO MAN: Valentino's ex-leading lady.

HOLLYWOOD: Oh, yeah, I mentioned her last week.

AUDIO MAN: Says to tell you she ain't a dope addict like you said, and is gonna slap you with a big fat libel suit....

HOLLYWOOD: Tell her to come on down here and slap me in the face instead! *(He laughs and starts to pack up.)* These cheap no-talents and out-of-the-way has-beens! They should be grateful I'm even mentioning them on my show or in my column at all! Gets them a lot of free publicity! Nita Naldi could get a movie contract right now if she wanted to—if she really ain't no dope fiend!

BETTY: HC — you don't actually believe....

HOLLYWOOD: What?... That I couldn't get her a contract if I tried? All's I'd have to do is lift a pinky and she'd be back in the spotlight....

BETTY: My God...

HOLLYWOOD: We're a hit, Betty, don't you understand? Since I began our Sin Purge, we got a radio show, and the ratings have gone through the

ACT TWO 73

roof! Three in ten people in this country are listening to Hollywood Confidential! Three in ten! We're on a moral mission, you and me, a mission to save this country from fairies and Reds! Say, did you talk to those folks at the *Saturday Evening Post?*

BETTY: I sure did. They — they asked all sorts of questions about you. Who are your favorite movie stars—

HOLLYWOOD: Rooney and Temple —

BETTY: Yes, of course — what are your favorite foods—

HOLLYWOOD: That pie you made for me at your place the other night, did you tell 'em about that?

BETTY: They even asked if you and I were going to be engaged!

HOLLYWOOD: The lady behind the man, huh, Betty? Maybe that's what they'll call the article!

BETTY: You're going to be late to that Legion of Decency dinner.

HOLLYWOOD: What about Hyde? Did you get a copy of his movie script?

BETTY: I told you. There are too many fake scripts around. Nobody knows which is the real one.

HOLLYWOOD: That's ridiculous! They've got to be shooting one of them, don't they?

BETTY: Yes, but it changes every day!

HOLLYWOOD: I want to see a script.

BETTY: It's impossible.

HOLLYWOOD: Nothing's impossible! I want to approve the script!

BETTY: Approve it?

HOLLYWOOD: I want you to go over there yourself.

BETTY: What?

HOLLYWOOD: Tell Hyde I want to know what he's putting in that picture, or I'll break all I know about him to the rest of the country.

BETTY: Look, HC, don't you think we've done enough with him—

HOLLYWOOD: Enough? People are saying he's making a picture about me!

BETTY: So what? He's already given us more information than....

HOLLYWOOD: There can never be enough, don't you understand? There can only be more and more! That's what this great nation's founded on, and when you're in like we're in, all we gotta do is TAKE, TAKE, TAKE! *(Pause)* God, I'm famished. Let's go eat. I need a steak!

BETTY: I — I don't want to go and see Julian Hyde.

HOLLYWOOD: YOU'LL GO! *(Pause)* I'm sorry.... Sometimes, I don't know what gets into me.... I'll go there myself....

BETTY: Oh, HC...

HOLLYWOOD: No. I'll go. *(Pause)* You're a peach, Betty. You know that?

BETTY: Am I?

HOLLYWOOD: Oh, yeah. A peach.

BETTY: And what about your girlfriends?

HOLLYWOOD: They ain't in the same market.

BETTY: What do you mean?

ACT TWO 75

HOLLYWOOD: You wouldn't pick them like you'd pick you. *(Pause)* You know, all these months...it's incredible what's happened, isn't it?

BETTY: It is incredible, HC....

HOLLYWOOD: And you know why it happened? Because you were with me. It's all because of you.... You are my good luck charm. I need you. You know what we're doing is right, don't you?

BETTY: Of course, HC, I just don't like it when we hit everybody so hard....

HOLLYWOOD: I know that, but sometimes we can't help it. We've got to stick by our principles. I— I can't have you being disloyal. Not now. Not when we're getting to be so big....

BETTY: No, HC...

HOLLYWOOD: I've never had that.... I've never had someone with me...to share my dreams.... It's lonely, sometimes.... Sometimes I get so lonely....

(HOLLYWOOD *moves to* BETTY. *They embrace.*)

HOLLYWOOD: Don't change, darling. Whatever you do...don't change....

(As if a dam has burst for her)

BETTY: I won't change, Herman....

(HOLLYWOOD *shudders as their embrace becomes more passionate.*)

BETTY: I won't change.... I can't help it....

(*Suddenly,* HOLLYWOOD *becomes manic.* BETTY, *scared, tries to stop him.*)

BETTY: Don't, HC... Not now...

(He holds her. He grabs her more violently.)

BETTY: Stop it, please... HC?... Stop...!

HOLLYWOOD: I'm sorry, Betty. I just...for a moment.... I'm sorry....

(BETTY *looks at* HC, *a horrified look on her face. Lights suddenly come up harsh in the sound booth, projecting weird shadows on* HOLLYWOOD's *face.*)

AUDIO MAN: We're finished, HC. Good night.

HOLLYWOOD: What? Oh...yes...good night...

(*Pause.* BETTY *stares at* HOLLYWOOD *for a moment.*)

HOLLYWOOD: I'm sorry, Betty.... I didn't mean....

(*Lights go out in booth.* BETTY *turns and leaves.* HOLLYWOOD *stands alone, in the shadows for several seconds.*)

HOLLYWOOD: Betty?... Betty?... Good night... *(Pause)* And good night, Shirley Temple, wherever you are....

(*Pause. Lights remain on* HOLLYWOOD's *face, as we hear:*)

LOUELLA PARSON'S VOICE: This is Louella Parsons in Hollywood.... Insiders are bickering over whether movie star Julian Hyde's new picture is really about gossip sensation Hollywood Confidential.... The irate columnist is trying to act casual, but Hyde's publicist won't confirm or deny... what skeletons are rattling, and in whose closet?

(*Lights rise on the screening room where* HYDE *and* HOCK *are watching rushes.*)

HYDE: Terrible! Awful! I can play this scene much better!

HOCK: Your face certainly looks frightening there.

HYDE: Not frightening enough!

HOCK: You want it to look more frightening?

ACT TWO

HYDE: Demonic. Possessed. Andrew?

ANDREW: We can try relighting it from the back.

HYDE: Forget it! I'll look angelic!

HOCK: You can't possibly look angelic! Not in this part!

HYDE: Enough! TURN IT OFF!

(Lights come up as rushes end. HYDE *paces as* HOCK *looks worried.)*

HOCK: What's the matter with the performance?

HYDE: I haven't gotten to the heart of the man. I'm still struggling to find him.

HOCK: You have found him. You've made him quite real — even touching, in places — I think what you've done so far is simply extraordinary.

HYDE: Thank God! Then you like it?

HOCK: Yes, yes, I like it! But it scares the pants off me! Here you are worrying about your performance, when the very picture you're making is going to blow us all to Kingdom Come! Hollywood Confidential wants approval of everything you're shooting!

HYDE: That's impossible! You think he's going to like what I'm saying about him?

HOCK: Of course not! Once he finds out what you're showing, he'll sue us for every inch of this studio.

HYDE: He can't prove anything.

HOCK: He doesn't have to, to close us down!

HYDE: It's a piece of fiction!

HOCK: Fiction? When you say he's blackmailing senators and movie stars, causing the suicides of powerful businessmen and making and breaking careers? And who's this girl you stuck in in the middle of the story?

HYDE: We now know there was a girl he loved very much, who broke his heart. But we haven't been able to find out anything more about her.

HOCK: Cut that girl out of the picture! Cut all references to her, and lose the eyeglasses.

HYDE: But I'm wearing them in everything we've shot so far!

HOCK: Then reshoot your closeups! I'm telling you, Julian, I'm not going to let you put this studio in jeopardy like that! You do as I say, or I won't release this picture, no matter what kind of a masterpiece it is!

HYDE: You...would do that?

HOCK: My word of God!

(Pause)

HYDE: Look, I know there've been a lot of problems — I'll solve my own performance — but that's how this picture's got to be made....

HOCK: This picture! Don't say another word about this picture! Everything in it is being written and rewritten based on what you and Singer are finding out every day about one man —

HYDE: That's because I'm fighting for my life with it!

HOCK: It's your life against an entire goddamn industry!

HYDE: An industry that's going to be ruled by this man if it doesn't start fighting back the way I am!

HOCK: It's already being ruled by him! My God, the things he's been digging up about people!? You think you can stop that?

ACT TWO   79

HYDE: I have to! I helped start it, didn't I? I made the deal — the deal you WANTED me to make, remember? You knew I'd have to sell my soul to him — and sell it I have!

HOCK: That's enough!

HYDE: I'll get him, Charley!

HOCK: You'll get him! And it will change the way the country thinks of him?

HYDE: It will change everything!

(HOCK *has gone to the telephone.*)

HYDE: What are you doing?

HOCK: Putting an end to this madness once and for all...

HYDE: Who are you calling?

HOCK: New York.

HYDE: You can't. If I go, you go. They'll fire you.

HOCK: What...?

HYDE: I'm all you've got left to defend yourself with. The only reason they're keeping you on is to see how our picture does. If you shut us down now, we've accomplished nothing....

HOCK: What are you talking about...?

HYDE: They know, Charley. They know...about your trips to the doctor.

(*Pause*)

HOCK: Do you remember Fred Ott?

HYDE: Who?

HOCK: Fred Ott. He sneezed and it changed my life. Edison's first picture. *Fred Ott's Sneeze*. Made eight or so years after I was born. My dad was manager of a clothing store in Oshkosh. I used to play the kinescopes all day long. Fred Ott. Little Egypt, who did Salome's Dance of the Seven Veils. The Keystone Cops in *Ton of Trouble*. Make people laugh, I thought. Make 'em laugh, or scare the hell out of them. I knew a good thing when I saw it.... Well, I've made a lot of people laugh, and scared the hell out of even more. I've built this studio up, and now, at the first chance, they're going to try and take it away from me!

HYDE: Let's show them, Charley. Let's show them we won't take this lying down....

(Pause)

HOCK: Henderson. The goddamn chairman of the board. He told me he loved my pictures.

HYDE: Love! There is no love in this business! Nobody does anything at this studio out of love!

HOCK: Julian...what are you saying?

HYDE: Why do we always want everybody to love us? Why is a business so in love with courage so frightened itself?

HOCK: You're changing.... You've changed....

HYDE: Maybe! I don't know! Something's happening inside me, and....

HOCK: It's Hollywood Confidential....

HYDE: No... It's me.... It's what's inside me....

HOCK: He's destroying you.

HYDE: I am destroying him!

HOCK: You are destroying yourself! *(Pause)* Lose the eyeglasses.

(HOCK leaves. HYDE stares out at the movie screen.)

HYDE: Could we run that scene again, please....

ACT TWO

(Lights dim in the room, and the flickering light starts.)

HYDE: *(On screen)* Fight me! Hit me! KILL ME! But I hate your petty little snivelling....

RICARDO: I will kill you, if I have to.... I swear, I will!

BABYLON: You can't kill me! You don't have it in you.... You may as well kill yourself....

(HYDE, watching, suddenly buries his face in his hands.)

ANDREW: *(Off)* That's all, Mr Hyde.

(The lights come up. HOLLYWOOD *is seated beside* HYDE.*)*

HOLLYWOOD: Quite a remarkable scene, Julian.

HYDE: My God...

HOLLYWOOD: You look terrific. But the hat isn't quite right. Here's something you might not know. When I talk on the radio, I always keep my hat on my head. Makes me talk faster, for some reason. Isn't that funny? *(Pause)* Am I proving interesting?

HYDE: Very. If slightly elusive.

HOLLYWOOD: Elusive? In what way? The stuff of American legend, I should think.

HYDE: Certainly would be if Eddie Harrell were publishing it. He might not mention the dirty little secrets you uncovered about your first editor that got you promoted from copy boy to columnist.

HOLLYWOOD: It was only one dirty secret, and it wasn't so little.

HYDE: Still, it started you on the road early.

HOLLYWOOD: If you knock somebody big, you get attention. If you print it, it never quite looks like a lie.

HYDE: That's been your credo from the very beginning, hasn't it? Well, maybe I can use it myself. I still know what the public wants.

HOLLYWOOD: I doubt the public wants the ideas of a degenerate. *(Pause)* You may be a talented man, Julian, but you are, and always will be, an outsider trying to fit in. You don't share the thinking of the mainstream of this nation.

HYDE: And you do?

HOLLYWOOD: I understand them a lot better than you.

HYDE: Do you know what's the matter with the mainstream of this nation? That it lets people like you tell it what heroes to idolize, only to tear them down when they fail to conform to vague moral standards it's impossible for any human being to uphold —

HOLLYWOOD: Moral standards like family? Motherhood? God? Decency?

HYDE: Those are mere symbols.

HOLLYWOOD: A nation lives by its symbols! Those symbols must represent the best in us!

HYDE: And you think you're what is the best in us?

HOLLYWOOD: I'm not a celebrity.

HYDE: You've turned yourself into one! A different kind of celebrity! And if I don't expose you, I'm sure one day soon there'll be somebody else who will!

HOLLYWOOD: We'll just have to see about that, won't we.... *(Pause)* I'm going to stop your picture. Listen to my broadcast Sunday night.

DAVID: *(Off)* Julian...?

(DAVID *enters.*)

HYDE: David! What —what are you doing here?

ACT TWO

DAVID: I told you I might be stopping by.

HOLLYWOOD: Hello, Mr Hogarth.

DAVID: HC. My God. Sorry, I didn't know you two were....

HOLLYWOOD: Don't mind me. I'll leave you boys alone. And Julian, in case you think I'm not serious.... Thanks for all your help. I really liked the scoop on Gable.

(HOLLYWOOD *leaves.* DAVID *and* HYDE *watch after him.*)

DAVID: Was that meant for me?

HYDE: I think so.

DAVID: Then he still doesn't know.... *(Pause)* You think he'll use the stuff about Laughton?

HYDE: I hope not.

DAVID: So do I. *(Pause)* I can't take much more of this, Julian.

HYDE: Would you rather I never told you?

DAVID: No. I'd rather we never had to do it in the first place. I hate going to my job. I feel like a horrible traitor. I think Mayer's going to start bugging the phones —

HYDE: Tell him to bug everything! Open the mail! Search the staff and inspect all the cars! We're none of us safe anymore! No one is safe!

DAVID: Julian...?

HYDE: You're right. Why did I ever get you involved?

(Pause)

DAVID: I think what you're doing is very brave. You're making your picture. Honestly. Without deception.

HYDE: Honestly! Without deception! We're betraying our friends!

DAVID: You're standing up to Hollywood Confidential! And when it's done, you'll have helped stop him!

HYDE: How? With a little machine that sends out flickers of light and tells people when to laugh and cry?! Pictures can't change life! Only life can change life! Real people! Real events! Wars! Laws! Elections! What we're doing is...playing with shadows, David.... Punching at shadows in the dark...

(Pause)

DAVID: After the picture is done, can we get out of here for a while?

HYDE: You mean, leave Hollywood?

DAVID: Can we do that?

HYDE: I'd like to go as far away as we can get.

(Lights quickly go down on them as we hear:)

HEDDA HOPPER'S VOICE: This is Hedda Hopper's Hollywood.... The drama at Hock Studios has heated up this week, as newspaper and radio personality Hollywood Confidential has tried to stop the filming of Julian Hyde's new motion picture, *The Rise and Fall of Harry Babylon*.... Why is Hollywood Confidential on the warpath? And what is Julian Hyde so afraid of? And will the rest of us ever find out?

(Lights come up on HYDE's office. ANDREW and CREW MEMBERS walk in along with JAKE.)

CREW: Why aren't we shooting?

ANDREW: Mr Hyde's been in Hock's office all morning.

CREW: But we're ready to shoot the final scene!

ACT TWO

ANDREW: I— don't know. Mr Singer?

JAKE: Don't ask me. He won't tell me what's going on. And I've written every ending possible except the eruption of Mount Vesuvius.

(BETTY *emerges from the office shadows.*)

BETTY: Mr Singer?

JAKE: Yes?

BETTY: Mr Hyde's secretary said I could wait here, as it was time for her to....

JAKE: What can I do for you?

BETTY: I work for Hollywood Confidential....

(*Pause*)

JAKE: Armstrong, isn't it? Miss Betty Armstrong?

BETTY: Why, yes... How did you —

JAKE: Tell Mr Hyde I need to see him. Immediately.

ANDREW: Yes, Sir.

(ANDREW *and the others leave.*)

JAKE: You're — you're prettier than I'd imagined.

BETTY: *(Flustered)* I — what? What makes you.... That's nice of you to say....

(*Pause*)

JAKE: I don't suppose you've come down to take a look around the studio?

BETTY: A look around? Oh. Well — no, not exactly...

JAKE: I'd be happy to show you my office, but it's nothing special. It looks out onto a lovely air shaft. After I'm gone I'm hoping they'll put up a plaque. (*Pause*) You're not here on your boss' behalf, are you.

BETTY: What — what makes you say that?

JAKE: I don't know. Just a hunch, I guess.

BETTY: You'd make a pretty good gumshoe, Mr Singer. If you ever decided to quit writing pictures.

JAKE: Please. Call me Jake. Let's be a little dangerous.

BETTY: I don't like danger. Jake.

JAKE: Somehow I don't believe that. And I already have. Decided to quit writing pictures, I mean. But not just yet. Because I have to help my friend finish this one.

BETTY: Very noble.

JAKE: Noble? No. Just professional. A screen hack doing my job.

(Pause)

BETTY: Do you know how Herman Buss began his career? He stole fifty dollars from his father's piggy bank and left Chappawick, Pennsylvania, hopping a bus for New York City. Went to work on a newspaper. Became a runner for the *Graphic*. You remember the *Graphic*? "Daily PhotoDrama from Life" with models posing in the studio. And the "Composograph," pictures made up of composites from other pictures. That's how Herman Buss began his career. Cutting out pictures of Rudolph Valentino, sticking him in the fake bedrooms of starlets he'd probably never even met.... *(Pause)* That was a long time ago, and Herman Buss was very young.... But he's been doing the same thing ever since....

JAKE: He doesn't treat you very well, does he? *(BETTY shakes her head.)* And you love him very much, don't you...?

BETTY: Have you ever loved somebody so much, that you only see the good things about them, and refuse to see the bad? Somehow the world becomes enlarged

ACT TWO

by this person in a way you never thought possible... and no matter what that person says, or does, you fall hopelessly under his spell.... *(Pause)* You see, the last few months have been a nightmare. Things have gotten much worse. I suppose I should have seen it from the beginning. But Herman has become truly terrifying. And as much as I love him, I know he needs to be stopped....

JAKE: And how do you propose we do that?

BETTY: With whatever information you may have. *(Pause)* The other day, I found this among some of HC's things.

(She hands something to JAKE.*)*

JAKE: What — what is this...?

*(*HYDE *enters, dressed as* BABYLON.*)*

HYDE: Jake, where are those new pages? We need them right away!

JAKE: Julian, this is Miss Betty Armstrong.

BETTY: My God...

HYDE: What is it?

BETTY: No, it's...just the way you...look....

JAKE: Miss Armstrong found something of yours. She thought you might be interested in it....

*(*JAKE *hands it to* HYDE. HYDE *looks at it.)*

HYDE: It's the ring. It's Lida's missing wedding ring. Where did you...? *(Pause)* My God...

(Lights go down on scene, and come up on HOLLYWOOD CONFIDENTIAL *in the radio booth, on the air.)*

HOLLYWOOD: Here in California, I will be happy to serve as co-chairman of a fact-finding committee on un-American activities along with Senator Tenney, and thank publishers Eddie Harrell and Willie Randolph Hearst for their courageous campaign of withering publicity against subversive elements in the state and the union.... We will fight to ban the Communist Party from the upcoming election ballot.... We will investigate all business takeover schemes of the rich bankers and moneylenders, and support nonintervention in the current world crisis....

(HOLLYWOOD *signs off as* ANNOUNCER *begins selling Lux Liquid.*)

HOLLYWOOD: Where the hell is Betty?

AUDIO MAN: Hasn't come back yet, HC.

HOLLYWOOD: What's taking her? That preview was supposed to be over by 8:30.

AUDIO MAN: It's only 9:15.

HOLLYWOOD: Somebody call that cockamamie theater in Encino and find out if they've left.

AUDIO MAN: Righto.

(*Phone rings in booth.* HOLLYWOOD *answers it.*)

HOLLYWOOD: Hello? Ernie!... Of course the show's going great.... Where's Betty? How's that Crawford picture they sneak previewed tonight?... What?... What do you mean, it wasn't a Crawford picture? *A Woman's Face*, ain't that the one?... What?... *The Rise and Fall of Harry*...but that's Hyde's picture!... — A sneak screening? He did WHAT? They SHOWED it!... Goddamnit! Stop talking so fast! The audience loved it? Who loved it? Who was there?... Warner?... Warner said it could be trouble?... Ernie, tell me what you're talking about!... What do you mean, it could be trouble...Ernie?...Ernie?! (HOLLYWOOD *puts phone down sharply.*) Goddamn idiot! Trouble! Nobody gives Hollywood Confidential trouble! Nobody! (*Phone*

ACT TWO

rings.) Sid! What the hell was Hyde's picture getting screened for? Who okayed that? What do you mean, I'll need a lawyer? I got millions of lawyers!... Implications?... What kind of implications?... I'm gonna talk to Zanuck about— HE was there, too? What do you mean, you gotta go? NOBODY'S GOTTA GO WHEN THEY'RE TALKING TO ME, SID!... Sid? *(Slams the phone down.)* GODDAMN IT! I KILLED THAT PICTURE! WHAT ARE THEY ALL TALKING ABOUT?... Get me Nick Schenck at Metro!

VOICE: Righto.

HOLLYWOOD: We gotta stop Julian Hyde!

(A figure appears. It is the FLORIST.*)*

FLORIST: Mr Confidential?

HOLLYWOOD: What — what do you want?

FLORIST: I was asked to bring you this.

HOLLYWOOD: What is it?

FLORIST: It's from Julian Hyde. Who says to tell you he thought you'd like it better than flowers....

(He hands the package to HOLLYWOOD.*)*

HOLLYWOOD: Julian Hyde... What the hell?... *(He opens it. It is a movie script.) Harry Babylon: His Rise and Fall...* The script to Hyde's movie. This is the.... *(A note falls out.* HOLLYWOOD *reads it.)* "I know you killed her. I have the ring." *(He freezes.)* Jesus... *(Phone rings.)* Nick! What the hell happened? You were supposed to stop Julian Hyde's picture!... It's inflammatory to a lot of people! There's blood on it, and there'll be more if something ain't done!... Listen, Nick, I'll have your job. I'll go right to the top. I want to talk to Mayer!... What do you mean, he won't talk to me!... Well, he damn well better talk to me, or I'll tell all I know about everybody at his Studio! Bastard! Goddamn! Tell him —Hello?... Hello?... Hello...?

VOICE: Stand by, Hollywood...

HOLLYWOOD: What?... No... Wait...

VOICE: In five, four, three, two...

(Pause. ON THE AIR light goes on. HOLLYWOOD approaches the microphone.)

HOLLYWOOD: My final note tonight, ladies and gentlemen... Uh... All of you kind, wonderful people out there... I think you all know how much I've enjoyed these broadcasts.... How much I DO enjoy them.... To come into each and every one of your livingrooms every Sunday night.... And into every bar and over every car riding the highways of this great nation of ours.... In all the hospital rooms and in the farmhouses and filling stations... What is it, do you think, that has made my talks with you so popular? I'll tell you what it is.... It is that deep inside you, you know there are deeper truths, higher truths which everybody else in the White House, in the press, at your jobs, in your town, even in your very own family doesn't want you to know.... There are questions which only have answers whispered from mouth to mouth, from lips to ears, and they are believed more firmly than anything Franklin Roosevelt or Louis B Mayer tells you.... What really happened to the Lindbergh baby?... What did Sacco and Vanzetti say just seconds before they died?... Who was at the party the night Fatty Arbuckle killed Virginia Rappe?... How many girls' babies did Charlie Chaplin really sire?... Who ran the presidency after Woodrow Wilson had his stroke?... How many Nazis have infiltrated Roosevelt's cabinet?... You wives think you know your husbands, but do you really believe all he tells you? Do you really trust his love and faith? You

ACT TWO

sons know your fathers, but do you really think all he says is true? Your village priest is celibate, but why does he catch your eye? Everything in this country has an appearance, but the reality behind the appearance is something else again.... Nothing is really what it seems.... From the most powerful person in this great nation of ours to the smallest, meekest, and humblest, there is deception, ladies and gentlemen.... Deception... The country is sick with such deception! A young girl comes to Hollywood with the dream of being a star, and she gets discovered on an opening night of a picture premiere, right outside of Grauman's Chinese Theater. She screen-tests, they color her hair, give her new clothes, and change her name.... And suddenly, she is a screen idol adored by millions of red-blooded American men. But who is she, really? Inside she is still that same scared little girl who came out West looking for love, but the only love she can find is the love of her fans who dream of her furtively in the dark.... She becomes just like all of them — and when somebody she loved tries to break through he is driven away, laughed at and told to disappear.... WELL HE WILL NOT DISAPPEAR! HE WILL EMPHATICALLY — NOT — DISAPPEAR!!... *(Pause)* I... Sorry, ladies and gentlemen... For a moment, I just.... False gods... We must fight the false gods that are threatening to devour us.... To devour me... There is one man in Hollywood tonight who is a false god.... He is a famous movie star, and he is a homosexual.... He corrupts the minds of your children in his pictures without you even knowing it.... Would you stop him if you could? He is evil. Hateful. He and his kind are a blot on the eye of God and a menace to the great tradition of the American family! Do you want to know who he is? Yes, Mr and Mrs America, of course you do.... He is Mr Julian Hyde.... That's right.... Julian

Hyde... The man whose pictures you've loved for over a dozen years.... The man some of you have thought about...dreamt about...wished you could meet.... You men out there have seen your girlfriends swoon over him, and ladies and gentlemen, he is not what he seems.... He is a fake, a degenerate masquerading as a noble, upstanding celebrity.... But we won't let him devour us, will we? No, we won't! We won't let him devour me! I am telling you the truth about him! He has deceived you, but I am bringing you the truth! I am bringing you the light! Do you know why you listen to me every week? You listen to me because I tell you the truth! I bring you the truth! I AM the truth! If it weren't for me, you'd sit in deepest despair and darkest ignorance, unable to cope with your sad, unhappy little lives.... I am the reason you can face the night, aren't I? I am the reason you can hold onto the dark.... I am the beacon by which you can see! All of you desperate, lonely people who want your lives to be as beautiful as the lives you see up on that screen.... As magical as the lives you read about in your movie magazines.... Well, their lives are no better than yours! Their dreams are no bigger! Their lives are all shadows and light! All shadows and light! Do not believe in them! Do not believe in M-G-M!

VOICE: It's time to sign off, Hollywood....

HOLLYWOOD: What...? Sign off...? I'm not signing off....

VOICE: Er — That's all for the Lux Ledger this week....

HOLLYWOOD: What? No! No... Ladies and gentlemen...

VOICE: Join us next week...

HOLLYWOOD: I'M NOT GOING OFF THE AIR! DO YOU UNDERSTAND? DO YOU HEAR ME? *(The closing theme drowns him out.* HOLLYWOOD *starts to scream.)* NO! WAIT! STOP! STOP! STOP!

ACT TWO 93

(Lights go down on him in the radio booth and up on HOCK's *office, immediately following. It is night.* HOCK, HYDE, JAKE, ANDREW, *and the lackeys from the first act are there.* HOCK *is on the phone.* HYDE *and* JAKE *are listening to* HOLLYWOOD *on the radio.)*

HOCK: He said he'd offer how much...? This is unbelievable!... Has he even seen the picture?... I understand.... If that's what the Board wants.... I'd have to get back to you.... Nick, there ain't even a lawyer here! Right... *(He puts down the phone.)* Mayer just offered more than half a mill to buy the picture.

HYDE: You don't mean buy it.

HOCK: Julian, I think you'd better leave....

HYDE: YOU MEAN, DESTROY IT!

HOCK: It's a ready cash deal, they're ordering me to do it....

HYDE: And all because Eddie Harrell will launch a hate campaign against the studios!

HOCK: For Chrissake, I TOLD you not to do this! I told you!

JAKE: But how can they bow to this pressure? The picture contains the truth.

HYDE: He murdered Lida.

HOCK: You have no proof —

HYDE: I don't need proof! I know he did it!

(Telephone rings. BUDDY *answers it.)*

BUDDY: Yeah?... Yeah... Sure... Hold on... *(To* HOCK*)* Nick Schenck again.

HOCK: Tell him I'll call back.

BUDDY: Says it's urgent.

HOCK: *(On phone)* Yeah, Nick... What?... My God... Yeah... I see.... Okay... Yeah... Bye... *(Hangs up)* The offer's withdrawn.

JAKE: What?

HOCK: The moguls have just begun to figure out what's happened. Support for Hollywood Confidential is crumbling.

HYDE: He never had support. It was power, plain and simple.

HOCK: They think he's gone crazy. He's been calling everybody in town, telling them he'll expose people and name names — they had to pull him off the air....

(The phone rings again. BUDDY on it.)

BUDDY: Yeah... Who?... Sure... *(To HYDE)* It's for you. From the radio station.

(HYDE takes the phone.)

HYDE: Hello?... Christ... Okay... *(Hangs up)* I'm going.

HOCK: Where?

HYDE: To get Hollywood Confidential.

JAKE: Where is he?

HYDE: Right out there. *(Points out window)* Standing on top of the HOLLYWOODLAND sign. Confessing to the murder of Lida Todd...

(Pause. HOCK and JAKE look at HYDE as the lights go down on the office. Sound of wind. In the darkness, we hear:)

REX: This is Rex Markum coming to you live. We interrupt Ben Bernie and his orchestra from the Fabulous Cocoanut Grove with a special news bulletin: A man reputed to be national columnist and broadcaster Hollywood Confidential has apparently

ACT TWO 95

climbed to the top of the Hollywoodland sign.... Several hundred have gathered beneath the sign.... We are standing at the bottom of the sign, and it looks like somebody is climbing up to get him.... I'm going to try to find out who —

VOICE 1: Who is it?

REX: Excuse me, can you tell me who the man is who is climbing up to the top of....

VOICE: It's Hyde! It's Julian Hyde!

(Sound of wind. The lights rise on the giant letters of the HOLLYWOODLAND sign—probably the first three or four letters. It is night, we are on top of a cliff overlooking downtown Los Angeles. Lights blink on and off in the distance. On top of one of these letters, HOLLYWOOD *shouts into the wind.)*

HOLLYWOOD: Our cause is America, our cause is freedom, and I can tell you better than anybody that I am what the American people want to hear! The President listens to me because he knows the people listen to me! Everybody in this hick town listens to me because they know the people and the President listen to me, and because they know their jobs won't be there in the morning if they don't.... Fear... This is what this town is built on.... Fear... Nobody can stop me! Nobody can hurt me! I am America and America is me! I am Hollywood and Hollywood is me! All this is mine! All this is me! I am the only thing here that...has no fear...no fear...no fear....

*(*HYDE *arrives, climbing up on the sign.)*

HYDE: Herman...? It's me...Hyde....

HOLLYWOOD: Julian...

*(*HYDE *arrives on top of sign.)*

HOLLYWOOD: Beautiful, isn't it? A night like this.

HYDE: Yes. Hard to believe that halfway around the globe, a madman is loose. We are at the dawn of a terrible new age.

HOLLYWOOD: Terrible? No. Wonderful. Look at all the blinking lights down there. And for every light a blinking hope. A tiny wish that I could grant. From Bette and Cary and Kate and Coop. My creations all.

HYDE: Do you really think that you created them...?

HOLLYWOOD: They all live in terror of what I will say or write...

HYDE: And tomorrow you will wake up and suddenly not be Hollywood Confidential anymore.... *(Pause)* Do you remember the last time you stood up here?

HOLLYWOOD: Would it matter if I did?

HYDE: Yes, it would matter. I finished everything in my picture. I shot my ending. The fall of Harry Babylon. Harry Babylon unmasked by his rival at the very place where he murdered the young starlet. Unmasked...and brought to justice.

(He shows HOLLYWOOD *the ring.)*

HOLLYWOOD: Lida...

HYDE: You loved her, didn't you...?

HOLLYWOOD: Yes...

HYDE: But she didn't love you back....

HOLLYWOOD: Oh, she loved me all right.... But she wanted to be a movie star, and she was afraid.... Afraid you'd never help her, if you knew she was already married. *(Pause)* We were going to be married in a tiny church in San Bernardino. Lucy was going to be a picture star, and I was going to be her director. Another Julian Hyde you'll be, she'd tell me. Another

ACT TWO 97

Julian Hyde. Well, she became the big star all right, and with none other than Julian Hyde himself....

HYDE: You were with her that night, weren't you? In front of Grauman's. The night I picked her out of that crowd....

HOLLYWOOD: For years I hated you not just because you'd changed her life...but because you didn't change mine....

HYDE: It's funny, what hate can do — it can purify things, make them clearer than ever before. When I dreamt about you at night, I dreamt about killing you, cutting you up, and eating you. About flinging you off the top of the Eiffel Tower on that soundstage across the lot. And then, when I'd wake up — I'd go to the studio and make a picture about you — a picture in which I could kill you without ever even laying a hand on you.... *(Pause)* That is what I could do to you that you could never do to me.

HOLLYWOOD: But you have failed. I've exposed you.

HYDE: It doesn't matter. I've made my picture. And it will live on — beyond me AND you.... Even if it cost me everything to make it!

HOLLYWOOD: What has it cost you?

HYDE: More than you know. I had to betray my friends to make it — and that will haunt me for the rest of my life! *(Pause)* Come with me, Herman.

HOLLYWOOD: What? No...

HYDE: You have to face up to what you've done. You killed her.

HOLLYWOOD: I killed Lida, not Lucy. Lucy was dead long before that. Dead by your hand. Yours and this town's. It was so quiet, when it happened. She — she wanted me to kill her.... She wanted Lida to die, so that Lucy could be finally set free....

(The crowd below starts to shout and cheer.)

HOLLYWOOD: Hear them? They want blood! MY blood! OUR blood!

HYDE: You're coming with me if I have to take you myself!

HOLLYWOOD: Then take me! Hit me! Kill me!

(HYDE goes for HOLLYWOOD; grabs him.)

HOLLYWOOD: We are bound together, you and I — bound together forever and ever!

(HOLLYWOOD lunges at HYDE. Grabs him. Starts to choke him. HOLLYWOOD slips. Starts to fall.)

HYDE: *(Shouts)* NOOOOOO!

(He grabs HOLLYWOOD to help him. They go over the cliff. Shouts and screams are heard. REX and others, including JAKE, have appeared.)

REX: They've fallen!

MAN #1: Where's Hyde? There! Down there!

BUDDY: Is he moving? I can't tell!

BOOKIE: One of them is still alive!

HOCK: Get some men down there....

REX: I am here talking to Mr Jake Singer.... Mr Singer, did you have any idea this was going to happen?

JAKE: It was in them from the beginning. Somehow it was in them from the start....

(As police sounds are heard, the HOLLYWOODLAND sign disappears. The stage becomes bare, with bright lights, flecked, shimmering, a sense of sunlight and water. The others disappear, JAKE last of all, as he stands alone for a

moment, and is replaced by MARTIN. *The scrim lights up and says: 1959. Lights rise on* HYDE, *now old, in a wheelchair, talking to* MARTIN *by the pool.)*

HYDE: Yes, it was in us from the start, all right! It was in us from the very beginning!

MARTIN: But you were the one who was saved....

HYDE: Oh, I was saved, yes....

MARTIN: And because Hollywood Confidential was dead, they released the damn picture, after all!

HYDE: Yes, they released it.... You'll make another picture, they said. After the talk dies down.... Well, the talk died down...and something in me died with it.... With him, I suppose...on that hill above Hollywoodland... The war came! The greatest horror of the century! I SAW HIM EVERYWHERE! And after it was over...it seemed my time, too, had passed...and I never made another picture again....

MARTIN: But the last one you did make.... A classic, Mr Hyde...

HYDE: Yes. A classic. I made a classic, goddamnit! But oh...what I lost to make it! *(Cries out)* LOOK. LOOK AT THESE LEGS. THIS IS WHAT I HAVE TO REMEMBER HIM BY!

(He throws aside his bath robe, revealing his legs to be wooden, hollow. HYDE *laughs. His laugh turns to a sob.)*

(Pause. It is early morning now. HYDE *looks at* MARTIN.*)*

HYDE: Have you talked to David?

MARTIN: He said — he would talk about it all only after you did....

HYDE: Dear David. He left Hollywood and never came back. Not once in twenty years....

MARTIN: He told me...he wanted you to go with him....

HYDE: Yes... But I couldn't.... What was it in me that didn't want to leave...? I wanted to remain here...as a reminder to them...as a reminder to them all.... And to myself... *(Pause)* Once, there was nothing more important to me than making motion pictures. And starring in them, of course. But over the years, I have come to demand less of the world, not more. Somehow it becomes easier that way. It is easier... when you give up trying to have such an effect upon the world.... And let the world begin to have some effect upon you.... *(Pause)* So do you have enough? For your book?

MARTIN: I — yes, I think so....

HYDE: Will you get a big fat advance and go on that TV show back in New York, late at night.... Who is it?

MARTIN: Jack Paar...

HYDE: Yes... You'll go on Jack Paar, won't you?

MARTIN: Maybe.

HYDE: How's your father?

MARTIN: Fine, I think. Writing. In England. They — they blacklisted him, you know.

HYDE: Yes. *(Pause)* The things men do to other men, Martin. That is the only real thing to write about today. *(Pause)* Almost light. Just what I'm waiting for.

MARTIN: How long have you been painting?

HYDE: Since I could hold a brush. But first light is still my favorite time of day. Cezanne liked to paint landscapes early in the morning. Do you know why? Because the light was at the right angle. The angle he desired. We both desired the right angles once, Cezanne and I. Only I desired many of them, one after the other. *(Pause)* Yes... Maybe I should.... It is going to be hot today, isn't it?

ACT TWO

MARTIN: Yes, Mr Hyde.

HYDE: And sunny. Look at the light. You can almost touch it. Look at the light.

(Pause. HYDE *holds up his arms as if touching the sunlight. The sun beats down upon them. The stage is bathed in light.)*

CURTAIN

www.ingramcontent.com/pod-product-compliance
Lightning Source LLC
Chambersburg PA
CBHW071721040426
42446CB00011B/2160